KT-502-884

MOURINHO

MOURINHO

Anatomy of a Winner

PATRICK BARCLAY

ORION

Copyright © Patrick Barclay 2005

The right of Patrick Barclay to be identified as the author
of this work has been asserted
by him in accordance with
the Copyright, Designs and Patents Act 1988.

First published in hardback in Great Britain in 2005 by
Orion Books
an imprint of the Orion Publishing Group Ltd
Orion House, 5 Upper St Martin's Lane,
London WC2H 9EA

1   3   5   7   9   10   8   6   4   2

All rights reserved. Apart from any use permitted under
UK copyright law, this publication may only be reproduced,
stored, or transmitted, in any form, or by any means, with
prior permission in writing of the publishers or, in the case
of reprographic production, in accordance with the terms
of licences issued by the Copyright Licensing Agency.

A CIP catalogue record for this book
is available from the British Library.

ISBN 0 75287 333 4

Typeset by Deltatype Ltd, Birkenhead, Merseyside
Printed and bound in Great Britain by
Clays Ltd, St Ives plc

Every effort has been made to fulfil requirements with regard
to reproducing copyright material. The author and publisher
will be glad to rectify any omissions at the earliest opportunity.

www.orionbooks.co.uk

Contents

PART FOUR
Behind the mask

Acknowledgements

It says much for José Mourinho that no one to whom I spoke in connection with this book – from such giants of the football world as Sir Bobby Robson and Louis Van Gaal to Andre Chin, whom Mourinho once taught at a school in Setúbal – had a bad word to say about him. Presumably he has had all his enemies shot.

To be serious: the man from Chelsea Football Club who told me Mourinho 'doesn't like people writing books about him without his permission' could have – and, I hope, did – put the great man's mind at rest. This was always going to be a legitimate study of a football coach and I am deeply grateful to those important figures in the game who, understanding its purpose, gave their time and insight so generously. Robson and Van Gaal apart, they included Gérard Houllier, David Moyes and the infectiously enthusiastic, profoundly influential Andy Roxburgh.

It was a joy to obtain the thoughts of Desmond Morris – fascinating, as ever – and to learn from my old friend Ian Ross that even a cynical old bastard can succumb to Mourinho's charm. Invaluable background material on the man and his ways came from *Jose Mourinho: Made in Portugal* (Dewi Lewis Media, 2004), which he wrote with Luis Lourenco. Perspective was supplied by Frank Clark and Peter Robinson, memories by Mick Martin, Ross Mathie, Tosh McKinlay and Gary Bollan. Thanks are also due to Andre Chin, Ian Aitken and several people who cannot be named because they might get into trouble with Mourinho; to Paulo Anunciacao and Christina Lamb; to David Luxton of Luxton Harris, who guided me towards the idea; to Ian Marshall, Ian Preece and Mark Rusher for their editorial sensitivity; and to a truly special one, Lauren Clark, for her patience and advice.

While writing the book, I was often asked if Mourinho had collaborated – I suppose people were wondering what he was like at close quarters – but I never sought that. For two reasons. Mainly that the publishers wanted my hands to be free to type as they chose. But also I wanted to keep all the money.

Patrick Barclay
August 2005

PART ONE

Welcome to England

He does what
it says on the tin

It was near the end of 2004, the year in which English football had encountered its most startling new manager since the first flush of Brian Clough.

As Christmas approached and the people on London's streets retained, for just a few more days, a blissful ignorance of the meaning, or indeed existence, of the word 'tsunami', a couple living in one of the more prosperous and fashionable districts of the capital decided to take their two children ice-skating. Every year a rink is created in a little square of shops just off the King's Road and, while it might cross a certain kind of mind to observe that the happy-family atmosphere engendered must be good for business, even such a cynic would find the remark freezing on pursed lips. For pre-Christmas crowds have a refreshing lightness of heart. Nuts and oranges may have given way to technological toys as the tokens of seasonal generosity, but the traditional spirit survives and, liberated by it, people reacquaint themselves with their best instincts in smiling at strangers or apologising when they might otherwise grimace. And our couple, to whom the experience of a Christmas in London was new, were obviously enjoying a rare afternoon as a family.

Each holding a child by the hand, they moved through the shoppers to the edge of the ice, where the girl and boy – she looked about nine years of age, he about five – were helped to put on their skates. Even muffled against the cold, the father attracted a few glances of recognition, but famous people, footballers among them, have often said that one of the benefits of coming to London is that they are not harried in the street and can live a relatively normal life (at least as normal as most of them would wish it to be), and this respect was accorded our man. One admirer took a photograph from such a distance that the subject would not have noticed. The only person who approached José Mourinho was a Portuguese football writer resident in London who knew him slightly and who, having wished him and his family a happy Christmas, withdrew to attend to his own wife and small son.

Mourinho leant back on a wall to watch as the boy and girl skated off, she confidently and he less so. When his view became obscured, Mourinho would walk off to check on them and usually, upon returning to his wife's side, he would kiss her. He frequently called to the children, encouraging them and, with signals, offering suggestions on how they could improve their technique. From time to time, like most of the other children, they fell and on one occasion the boy had difficulty in rising from the ice. Immediately Mourinho was with him, offering not a helping hand but a demonstration of the best method of getting up. He waited while the boy followed his advice, smiling patiently, not hurrying him. And off the boy went again, with more assurance than before. Anyone who saw the incident would have formed the impression that Mourinho was a good father. Which in turn provides a hint as to why he has made such an extraordinary impact on football. For at the highest level of management these days – and henceforth we shall fall into line with most of the rest of the world and refer to Mourinho's field as coaching – good fathers have taken over from the godfathers of old.

'I like the look of Mourinho,' Clough had said shortly before he died in September of that year. 'There's a bit of the young Clough about him. For a start, he's good-looking . . .' Which indeed Clough had been in his early days at Derby, before the booze began to blur his sharp features and mottle his complexion. But times have changed and you cannot boss a player around as easily as Clough might have done, or use the discipline of estrangement from his peers by sending a star to train with the youth team, as Clough once did. Most coaches have to accept that Sir Alex Ferguson, who can lash out at a stray boot and send it flying through the dressing-room air, drawing blood from one of David Beckham's expertly plucked eyebrows – and proceed, with total impunity, to sell the England captain to Real Madrid – represents the end of the line. One by one, culminating in the European Court case won by Jean-Marc Bosman in December 1995 that allowed players to move freely at the end of their contracts without their new employers having to pay a transfer fee, the constraints have been stripped away.

To claim that Ferguson and his predecessors in the English game – the likes of Sir Matt Busby at Manchester United, Bill Shankly and Bob Paisley at Liverpool, Don Revie at Leeds, Bill Nicholson at Tottenham and even Clough at Derby and Nottingham Forest – were mere martinets would be as misleading as to imply that Mourinho and Arsène Wenger, the most successful exponents of the modern style of coaching in England, have been indulgent softies. It would also do an injustice to the multi-dimensional nature of the job. Aime Jacquet, who coached France to victory in the World Cup in 1998, touched on this when he said: 'Today children are more curious and bolder. That is why we have to prepare coaches not just to teach youngsters about what happens on the pitch but about psychology, physiology, drugs, doping and social education. The coach of the future will have to be at different times a teacher, a buddy, a father, a friend, etc. It will not be enough for him simply to impose authority. He will need above all the ability to listen and pass on a message. He must be credible and able to defend his values.'

You may think those words a reasonable description of the role of today's youth coach, not applicable to those charged with guiding the aristocrats of modern football who earn their livings with Mourinho at Chelsea. Until you remember that during his first few months in charge of the club's expensively assembled squad he had to deal with the distraction created by the Romanian attacker Adrian Mutu's cocaine problem. Eventually, Mourinho ran out of patience. Mutu was tested by the club, sacked, named and shamed and, after a spell in limbo, went back to Italy, from whence he had come with notions of self-improvement. The message was clear: cross Mourinho, abuse the friendship of this buddy, and the only way is out. The modern coach must strike a balance between strength and sensitivity. Mourinho contrives to be both things to all men. That is part of the reason he is – to use his own word – special.

Should he have said it? Should he have breezed into England and inspired a classic *Sun* headline – 'The Ego Has Landed' – by telling the press Chelsea could be champions because they had terrific players and a 'special one' as coach? His own justification, outlined at the end of the season in a BBC television interview with Gary Lineker, was that he had suddenly found himself in a strange environment being showered with questions by people who seemed to be hankering for his credentials. Anyway, it was a statement of fact that he offered them rather than a grandiloquent aspiration; there are not many coaches who have won the UEFA Cup and Champions League in their first two full seasons with a club, sweeping up a couple of national championships and a domestic cup along the way, but that is what Mourinho had done with Porto in his native land.

At the culmination of all his achievements with the club from the football-steeped city by the Douro, sitting at a long table in the media centre of the stadium in Gelsenkirchen, Germany, where the Champions League final was won, he had spoken of his need for a fresh challenge. He had spoken with ambition and, over-whelmingly, of himself, and perhaps it was because of this that I, along with other journalists in England, got off on the wrong foot. It was not that his achievements could be belittled, more that the history of football was strewn with instances of success through chemistry – Arrigo Sacchi developed the formula for a great Milan, but nothing as explosive afterwards – and it looked as if this Mourinho chap was sorely tempting fate. The press were not alone in wondering if his pride came before a fall. The coaches waiting to pit their wits against him in the Premiership felt it too. One of the brightest, David Moyes, who was also to enjoy an outstanding season as Everton qualified for the Champions League by finishing fourth, recalls relishing the prospect of Mourinho's come-uppance. 'The initial feeling,' Moyes told me some months later, with a smile and a sigh, 'was that you just couldn't display that kind of arrogance in this country and get away with it. I think there were a few queueing up, you know, waiting to have a crack at him.'

We the professional bystanders did not hesitate to have fun with him. Such was his self-absorption (I wrote) that he would fit perfectly into contemporary London. I imagined him cutting a swathe through the traffic in a massive black 4x4 with smoked windows which, having stopped and carefully straddled two parking bays in order to reduce the risk of scratches from other vehicles, would disgorge the smooth operator, suit miraculously uncreased and mobile-phone cord dangling from one ear as details of the next day's training were laid down to a distant underling.

Well, I didn't know he was kind and attentive to his children, did I? I didn't know he would nuzzle his wife by the ice-rink wall when no one was looking. I didn't know he would treat the players with such sensitivity, and even charm the press. I didn't know the country would take such a liking to Mourinho that, by the Christmas of 2004, it could be asserted that he was the most admired football personality among neutrals and followers of his own club alike: a position that had fallen vacant because Newcastle had seen fit to part company with Sir Bobby Robson, Mourinho's old boss and guide.

Far from tempting fate with his high self-esteem,

Mourinho had taken fate in his hands and, as in Portugal, shaped it. I think that is the main reason we warmed to him: to borrow the brilliant simplicity of those television commercials for Ronseal, a range of products including varnish and woodstain, he does what it says on the tin. In England we have become used to a culture of inefficiency or, to use the expression favoured by football folk, sloppiness. When a train turns up on time, we are pathetically grateful. When we arrive home with a bag of oranges, tear the netting apart and find every single one rot-free, we almost burst into tears of joyous relief. Things go wrong, sometimes horribly wrong. Hideously wrong. At the time of Mourinho's arrival, anyone who emerged from a public hospital no worse than when he or she went in was assumed to have supernatural powers. Nor was this the only cause for public dismay. A war was conducted on the basis of 'intelligence' used without due care and attention. Small wonder that, in the build-up to the general election of May 2005, the key issue was to be identified as not health or education or security so much as the ability of any of the parties to deliver any promise at all. So little could be taken on trust. For many people, life in England had become a matter of hoping for the best.

Even in football, an activity rare in that it still inspired unrealistically high expectations, the customers' charter could not be relied upon to guarantee same-day delivery: why, the poor dears who supported Manchester United and Arsenal, the clubs who had established a clear superiority over all others since the Premier League was formed in 1992 (or the top division of the old Football League hived off and rebranded, as some of us might insist), had been obliged to share the intoxicating nectar of supremacy with each other. It was a cruel era in football. The language of the phone-in had become prevalent. Coaches of clubs from Tyneside to the south coast lost a couple of matches in succession and were decried for having lost much more than that; they had lost 'the plot'. In front of packed houses, the majority of teams 'underachieved'. Leeds United and others ran up vast debts 'chasing the dream', egged on by fans who, when the dream turned out to be a financial nightmare, immediately accused the directors of reckless extravagance.

Chelsea were among those who lived beyond their means in the early years of the 21st century. Until a small proportion of the riches Roman Abramovich had made – through Boris Yeltsin's shameful car-boot sale of the Russian people's oil and gas, let us never forget – was applied to an eminently unworthy cause, the saving of a football club's skin. The saving, moreover, of a club that had reached the verge of ruin under Ken Bates. To give Bates his due, that was the condition in which he had found Chelsea in the first place, and he left it much more robust than had been the case a quarter of a century earlier, when he was able to buy it for £1. But the advent of Abramovich still rendered Bates the luckiest man in football and, having taken the near-£20 million the Russian gave him for his shares and tried to settle in Monte Carlo, he soon got bored and returned to England to apply his unique abilities to the erstwhile dream-chasers of Leeds.

Chelsea were, on the face of it, even luckier. They had been plucked from the jaws of bankruptcy and turned overnight into the world's richest club. While Claudio Ranieri stayed as coach for one more year, clinging to his dignity with one hand and a negotiating position with the other, Peter Kenyon, the chief executive Abramovich had lured from Manchester United, courted the England coach, starting at what we can only presume he mistook – rather in the manner of an inexperienced mountaineer – for the peak of the profession. It was just a ridge. Kenyon, too, had a stroke of luck then for, when Sven-Göran Eriksson went to see him in his London flat, a newspaper photographer's prying lens was trained on the semi-transparent curtains. Once Kenyon and Eriksson had been caught together, the Football Association had a clear duty. Or so many of us thought. But, instead of indicating to the country that they could hardly afford to stand in the Swede's way, they gave Eriksson a cuddle and pay rise and Kenyon had to look elsewhere.

He now looked in the obvious place: the Champions League, where the forty-one-year-old Mourinho and the even younger Didier Deschamps, whose Monaco were to knock Chelsea out of the competition in the semi-final, were working their wonders on limited resources. He went for Mourinho, who, from then on, began working his wonders on unlimited resources. First Mourinho talked a good game. Then his Chelsea team played one. His implicit promise of the earth was about to be delivered. Just as it had been at Porto. He was doing what it said on the tin marked 'special'.

Why else did we like him as we shopped for Christmas in 2004? Many Arsenal supporters felt they had reason to thank him because he kept putting one over on Sir Alex Ferguson. At the same time there were United fans who simply liked the fact that he was not Arsène Wenger. Neutrals were grateful for a disturbance of the none-too-cosy duopoly that had ruled English football for twelve years with scarcely an interruption. They thought he might spice up the so-called mind games between Ferguson and Wenger, which were getting tedious in a way all fans of television soap opera would have found familiar. There were other factors in his popularity, including his looks – I mean: lots of people have a nice smile, and Mourinho's would melt ice, but he even has a nice scowl – and that indefinable quality which inspires curiosity. Why, I remember people asking at Christmas parties, does such a dapper man not shave before being interviewed on television after matches? Why does he leave his tie slightly loose?

So much for the tittle-tattle of a celebrity-obsessed age.

Mourinho had also been disarming his fellow coaches, the faces of the English footballing establishment, who had called him arrogant when he first came but who now grinned when you uttered his name and spoke with an affection not normally accorded the ridiculously advantaged. 'His team became so good so quickly,' said David Moyes, 'that you just had to admire him. He instilled such confidence and belief in his team and, while that's easier when you have top players, he did it at Porto too. So you could see that he'd earned his stripes, come up through the ranks and deserved to be in this top job.' All over the country coaches warmed to Mourinho, albeit with an air of slight bemusement; they noted aspects of his methods while admitting that the whole package defied analysis because he kept getting so much right and so little wrong. Even Ferguson and Wenger had their recurrent weaknesses; neither, to take a common instance, appeared capable of distinguishing a top-class goalkeeper from a cheese-and-tomato sandwich. Mourinho, having resuscitated the career of Vítor Baía at Porto, arrived at Chelsea at the same time as the best keeper from the European Championship, Petr Čech, and, after initially deciding to start the season with the man in possession, the much-respected Carlo Cudicini, had a late change of mind on the evidence of pre-season performances and promoted the newcomer; before long, Čech was to set a Premiership record by going 1,025 minutes without conceding a goal.

Underneath it all, I suppose, we were still waiting for Mourinho to fall. Not maliciously but out of curiosity. To see if the tin split. To discover what was inside it.

Blippin' marvellous

So after the Christmas of 2004 was past and people, having given with enormous generosity to tsunami-relief funds, returned to life's trivia, the occasional threat to Mourinho's status in our football-oriented society arose.

Towards the end of January it was reported that Mourinho, with Kenyon and two agents – so hazardous had football's waters become, it appeared, that even the agents were going around in pairs – had gathered in a London hotel room with Ashley Cole. The Arsenal and England left-back had two and a half years left on his club contract at the time and was therefore not allowed, under Premier League regulations, to meet a prospective new employer without permission from his current bosses: 'tapped', as the vernacular would have it. Arsenal clearly did not want to lose one of the more important members of Arsène Wenger's squad and were acutely displeased. Mourinho tried to dance out of discomfort, quipping that he had been in Milan on the day in question with Adriano (Internazionale's Brazilian striker, with whom, we were left to presume, Mourinho had been linked by the Italian press), but the joke fell flat on its face.

A few days later, Chelsea's doctor, Neil Frazer, left the club. Although the reason was officially given as ill health, he had incurred Mourinho's displeasure on several occasions.

Then the Cole allegation was revisited, the *Sun* producing a witness, a twenty-four-year-old room-service waiter called Ray Mason, a fine specimen of a breed unique to the English tabloid landscape in that he spoke almost entirely in fluent journalese. Mourinho, Mason claimed, had been rude to him, waving him away without a word when he tried to lay a plate. 'It wasn't until later,' Mason added, 'that I realised the enormity of what I had seen – a dodgy meeting that could blow the Premiership race wide open.' He alluded to Chelsea's substantial lead in the race, the implication being that, if the Premier League were to dock points from Chelsea as a punishment, Manchester United and Arsenal might be allowed back into serious contention for the title. However, although the Premier League appointed a retired judge to conduct an inquiry into the affair, no one acquainted with the politics and practice of football was ever in the slightest doubt that Chelsea would receive a fine, which turned out to be £300,000, and a warning in the form of a three-point deduction, suspended for a year.

Mourinho was fined £200,000 and later appealed; Cole was relieved of £100,000.

Their crime, in truth, was to be found out; most clubs 'tap' prospective signings in one way or another, usually through an intermediary, who might be a fellow player or even a journalist. And what, pray, had Kenyon been doing with Eriksson that night when the snooping snapper caught them through the curtains? The Football Association saw no value in an inquiry into their own employee's behaviour. This Premier League stance smacked of government by show trial. In any case, Chelsea dropped their supposed interest in Cole with alacrity.

One of the agents, Pini Zahavi, had been doing much of their business since Roman Abramovich took over (the other present in the hotel, Jonathan Barnett, was Cole's man). And Zahavi was to figure in another significant episode when, two months after the Cole affair came to light, the ubiquitous Kenyon was found to have hob-nobbed in London restaurants one Saturday night with Manchester United's Rio Ferdinand – another client of Zahavi, who was also there. Ferguson seethed and Wenger tartly observed that it was 'like seeing the same movie twice'. Except that Mourinho was now at a distance from the villain's role. While Kenyon protested his innocence, Zahavi stressed that Ferdinand was anxious to stay at United – if only his salary of £70,000 a week could be raised to something more like £120,000 –

without dispelling Sir Alex Ferguson's suspicion that his heart was already moving south. Kenyon tried to wipe the fresh mud off his sharp suit. None had stuck to Mourinho.

Rather more significant were events on boggy fields during the long, wet remainder of this winter of 2004–05. We had been waiting for Chelsea to encounter some adversity. The majority of people were not especially anxious that their Premiership lead be damaged – the most likely challengers, after all, seemed to be Manchester United, for whom little love was to be found outside their own vast global family – but we had a curiosity about how Mourinho and his charges would deal with it. The word most frequently used was 'blip', which was appropriate because Chelsea had been winning with the monotonous regularity of a healthy heartbeat, and the prelude to the week beginning on Sunday, 20 February featured much speculation that this might be the time. Mourinho duly announced he would send a weakened team to Newcastle for the FA Cup tie on that day, explaining that his key players – the likes of John Terry, Frank Lampard and Damien Duff – were not 'Supermen' and would have to be rested in readiness for the even more important Champions League first leg in Barcelona three days later.

Given that the week or, to be precise, period of eight days was to culminate in a Carling Cup final against Liverpool in Cardiff that would present Chelsea with an opportunity to take their first trophy under Mourinho, many felt he had little option but to rotate his players. He chose to blame the FA for making Chelsea play so late in the weekend prior to a Champions League week (and had a point, for all the Spanish and Italian contenders for Europe's biggest prize, including Barcelona, had finished their domestic matches by Saturday night), but it was a useful test for his expensively assembled reserves and they failed it. With Chelsea a goal down at half-time in the Tyneside sleet – the conditions were so inclement Mourinho had abandoned his customary grey cashmere coat for something more suited to a ski slope – he gambled by sending on all three of his permitted substitutes in the shapes of Lampard, Duff and Eidur Gudjohnsen. Within a few minutes Wayne Bridge had been carried off with a broken ankle. Chelsea, unable to equalise despite an improved level of performance, lost another man when their goalkeeper, on this occasion Carlo Cudicini, was sent off, leaving them with nine players, two of whom, Duff and William Gallas, were limping as a result of collisions and rated doubtful to start at Barcelona.

In the previous match, a Premiership visit to Everton, the home side had been reduced to ten men early when James Beattie foolishly butted Gallas, helping Chelsea to overcome an obstacle that was expected to be one of their more difficult on the road to the title. Mourinho, when it was put to him that Sir Alex Ferguson had cited this as an example of luck, replied, in a tone that affected surprise: 'No. I don't feel that. Because Beattie made a big mistake. He deserved a red card. If he had not deserved a red card and the referee showed him one, yes, I'd say the luck was with me.' This kind of logic, upon which, in my experience, every single successful coach is able to call at will, demands a great deal of thought. Could it now, I wondered, be applied to Mourinho's misfortune? Had he suddenly become, to paraphrase Napoleon, an unlucky general? Or, even worse, had he unnecessarily exposed players to injury with a mad gamble that would leave them debilitated in Barcelona and, perhaps, Cardiff?

Whatever the truth of the matter, we looked to the bench for a slippage of composure. We saw Mourinho congratulate his Newcastle counterpart, Graeme Souness, a few seconds before the final whistle and then, having walked on to the pitch, first console his own players then shake hands with several of their conquerors. He had performed this last act of sportsmanship before, but never, surely, in such circumstances. Interviewed afterwards, he said he was proud of his players, tendered a compliment to the referee, Mark Halsey, and added that he hoped Newcastle would continue to progress to the FA Cup final.

Such dignity was not only inherently pleasant but efficacious in applying a bandage to Chelsea's wound, and it occurred to me that Arsène Wenger could have done with a touch of the same at Old Trafford earlier in the season. There, you may recall, Arsenal were put out of their stride by Manchester United's unedifyingly harsh tackling – to be precise, that of the Neville brothers on José Antonio Reyes – and a couple of refereeing decisions. The so-called Battle of the Buffet ensued, during which Arsenal players threw food at Ferguson and the managers became embroiled in a furious confrontation. Arsenal's season was never quite the same again. Not for a few months anyway. It was still pretty good by the standards of most clubs, but soon they began to lose their grip on the Premiership title and had to be content with a fortuitous victory over United in the FA Cup final. Was this because Wenger had let them be burdened by the baggage of Old Trafford? True, the circumstances were different at Newcastle – Mourinho had no one but himself to blame, no outrage to absorb – but he was certainly not going to let a similar loss of momentum occur if he could avoid it. He would not countenance a turning point. He called upon his principles and looked forward, concentrating on the players who would do duty in the Camp Nou.

When the Chelsea party landed in Barcelona, it looked as if Mourinho was in top form. He went to the official press conference the day before the match and, without prompting, said he would announce not only his team – there were gasps, because at this level a coach never shows his hand in advance – but Barcelona's too. And he duly did, throwing in the name of the referee for good measure. The referee's name was Anders Frisk. We were to hear much more of it and this time Mourinho could not evade the mud. But for now the surprise of the assembled media representatives was mixed with amusement at Mourinho's latest antic. As for what the players must have thought of such a bold departure from convention, I was reminded of something the former Newcastle manager Arthur Cox once told me, when I came across him reading a biography of Montgomery of Alamein. 'Footballers,' he said, 'are like soldiers. They love their generals to be a bit eccentric, like Cloughie. It gives them something to talk about, binds them.' As for the rest of us, we had been charmed like cobras. We sank into our baskets and wished away the nagging reservations aired by the author of an editorial in the Spanish newspaper *AS*, who had said of Mourinho, after listening to his boast of having won as many European titles in his relatively short time at Porto (one) as Barcelona had done in their entire history: 'Although he won many trophies in Portugal, there were too many bad manners shown to opponents and too many dirty tricks. He has continued that at Chelsea.'

No doubt the author of those sentiments smiled in vindication as Duff, who had not been among the names listed by Mourinho, ran out at the Camp Nou. The explanation that the Irishman's recovery had been quicker than expected was received sceptically. But the fall from grace was only beginning. At half-time, with Chelsea leading 1–0, the teams were heading down the tunnel when the Barcelona coach, Frank Rijkaard, approached Frisk and said he felt Chelsea's goal should have been disallowed for offside against Duff. This was an inaccurate observation made in the wrong way at the wrong time and the Swedish referee told him so. But it was not as wrong as Chelsea's subsequent imputations against Frisk. An allegation that Rijkaard had been witnessed leaving Frisk's room was scorned (even by the English press, who, though they do love a drama, especially if it involves a wily foreign villain or two, also pride themselves on being able to spot a false claim from a mile away). A jaundiced eye also met Mourinho's implication that Frisk had proceeded to favour Barcelona by sending off Didier Drogba, who was shown a second yellow card for having raised his foot in challenging the goalkeeper. Down to ten men again, Chelsea had been unable to stem the flow of Barcelona attacks and lost 2–1.

Now Mourinho was not so cocky. He refused to attend the post-match media conference and instructed his players not to give any interviews either. Meanwhile Chelsea leaked the allegation about Rijkaard and Frisk and promised to lodge an official protest with UEFA, the governing body of European football. Since, from the moment of Mourinho's appointment, Chelsea had been indivisible from his image, it was he who bore the brunt of it. For the first time, he was not being taken seriously.

He had returned to the city where, under Bobby Robson and then Louis van Gaal, he used to work, undoubtedly one of football's capitals, and behaved in a manner that made him appear provincial. His peevish flouncing was a hark back to the great divide between Oporto and Lisbon, which all too often manifests itself in suspicion that a referee has either been bought or is giving the rub of the green free of charge. Mourinho's president during the great revival of Porto, Jorge Nuno Pinto da Costa, encouraged this. It is a far from exclusively Portuguese phenomenon. A similarly paranoid atmosphere has been observed in other small ponds inhabited by big fish: Scotland comes to mind. But there was another plausible reason, which arose in a conversation I had with Van Gaal, why Barcelona should have been the place where Mourinho went too far. Although Mourinho would probably not admit it, he had unfinished business with the Catalan club. For all that his years there gave him the perfect grounding for a top coach, Mourinho was often treated almost dismissively in Barcelona, referred to among the club's large media entourage (and even by some within the club) as 'The Translator'. This may help to explain his otherwise gratuitous-sounding reminder that he had won as many European titles as Barcelona. It may even excuse that. It hardly justified his dragging of Frisk into the crossfire of the ensuing battle.

So the form of defiance Mourinho chose did his

reputation no favours and he was to pay for it with banishment from the dugout and dressing rooms during each leg of the next Champions League contest, against Bayern Munich. It could, of course, have been argued on his behalf that the purpose of his post-match behaviour in the Camp Nou had been to deflect attention from the failure of his team to adjust tactically to Drogba's dismissal. If so, it was a ploy in which only a Machiavellian – 'in order to keep his people united and faithful,' wrote Machiavelli, 'a prince must not be concerned with being reputed as a cruel man' – would have taken great pride.

Nor did Mourinho distinguish himself on the eighth day. He became the most prominent figure in a cup final, and for a coach to assume that role, as Paul Hayward sharply observed in the *Daily Telegraph*, was about as appropriate as for a referee to do so. It was Sunday, 27 February and Chelsea's opportunity in Cardiff was to win the Carling Cup. By overcoming Liverpool at the Millennium Stadium they could lay hands on their first trophy of the epoch and, while gripping that emotionally precious metal, more acutely sense the comforting notion of Mourinho as Midas. Again, however, the coach saw much to ruffle him on the pitch and was animated as his men strove to cancel out a goal which John Arne Riise had quite beautifully struck on the volley in the first minute with the assistance of Chelsea marking loose enough to raise a statue's eyebrows.

A quarter of an hour from what might have been the final whistle came assistance from Steven Gerrard, the Liverpool captain who had nearly joined Chelsea the previous summer; endeavouring to assist his defence, he headed into his own net. Mourinho rose from the bench and, smirking, put a pointed index finger to his lips, as if to say 'Shush'. A section of Liverpool supporters behind him took offence and Mourinho, on the advice of the fourth official, Phil Crossley, was escorted down the tunnel. He went to the Sky television room, where, in a state of extreme agitation, he watched the thirty minutes of extra-time, during which a 3–2 victory was secured. He emerged for the presentation of the trophy and medals and resumed his habit of approaching the players of both sides. After congratulating his men, he toured the dejected Liverpool ranks, coaches, backroom boys and players, including Gerrard, whose hand he clutched and face he sympathetically cupped; Gerrard responded with a pat on the ribcage. Mourinho was enjoying himself hugely and the thought did occur, not for the first time, that here was something that set Mourinho apart from his fellow coaches: while most of them react to the final whistle by making for the dressing rooms, his instincts take him in the opposite direction. Might he, in gravitating towards the pitch, be seeking his share of the limelight he could never attract as a player?

Maybe it is not quite as simple as that. Maybe; he does love footballers as a breed and is genuinely drawn to their presence. But, in essence, the answer is yes. Mourinho is a performer. There is a passage in the book he produced with his journalist friend Luís Lourenço about how, when he returned to Benfica as Porto coach, he milked the abuse of a huge crowd before the match: 'I made a point of walking on alone, before the team . . . It was fantastic, an amazing feeling. I had never been a first-class player who could feel, for example, what Figo had felt upon returning to Barcelona [with Real Madrid], and so I had no idea what it would be like to have 80,000 people whistling and jeering at me. I believe that, when we are mentally strong, those people who seek to intimidate and disturb us have exactly the opposite effect. Upon hearing the whistles and jeers . . . I felt as if I were the most important person in the world.'

Anyone seeing him amid the more congenial atmosphere of the Millennium Stadium that late afternoon – most of the Liverpool supporters had drifted away, leaving the steep slopes to the hordes of blue-bedecked celebrants – would have thought him a happy man indeed. Yet behind the serenity of his smile was a grievance waiting to emerge and the post-match interviews provided the ideal opportunity.

The first questioner to confront him was Sky's pitchside man, Geoff Shreeves, who, after the routine on-camera pleasantries (in which Shreeves inquires as to how big a win it is and the triumphant coach, without being able to quantify it in cubic centimetres, says he is delighted for the club and the supporters), asked Mourinho if he regretted the behaviour that had led to his banishment from the arena. 'I don't regret,' he replied. 'I have a lot of respect for Liverpool fans and the signal was not for them. It was for the English press.' Balderdash. But he had hinted at a problem with journalists before the match, accusing them of increasing the stress of expectation on Chelsea by mentioning the money the club had spent on players. Such bizarre complaints scarcely register with press or public and are, in any case, primarily intended for consumption by the complainant's players as a motivational device. The unusual development here was that Mourinho was also looking for a confrontation with Sky, who are not usually regarded within football as mischievous (and have sound commercial reasons for wanting to maintain that reputation). Addressing Shreeves directly, as if holding the pitchside reporter responsible for every utterance of every commentator and analyst employed by Rupert Murdoch's organisation, he asserted: 'In my opinion you try to do everything to disturb Chelsea.' He had watched Sky's coverage of a Premiership match the previous day, in which Manchester United, by beating Portsmouth, had cut Chelsea's advantage over them to six points. 'You spoke more about Chelsea than Manchester United and, because the gap was cut, the sun shone.' When Shreeves responded that he sounded like a man under pressure, Mourinho flatly denied it.

So much for the dignity he had exuded at Newcastle a week earlier – and for which he had been praised by the Sky presenter Richard Keys. Once again we had seen the Porto mentality, the belief that the media would take one side or another for sinister reasons rather than, by loose consensus, arrive at the typically English notion – presumably expressed by the commentator at Old Trafford that Saturday when United won – that the result would add interest to the title race.

Often the top coaches are more pleasant in defeat than victory. Arsène Wenger is an exception, but Sir Alex Ferguson can accept adversity with good grace. The Scot can also turn a moment of vindication into a weapon and that is what Mourinho did in Cardiff. What a week it had been. He had maintained his reputation as a winner despite having encountered the blip, but along the way lost a little of his allure. The fact that he was tucked out of sight while his players were scoring the goals that took the Cup to west London was noted. The *Daily Mirror*, for so long a sorry example of the thing that ain't what it used to be, echoed its glorious past with a picture of the Chelsea players and the headline: 'They won it – he lost it.'

The perception of Mourinho had subtly altered. There were echoes here of what had happened to England's first foreign coach. When the FA had appointed Sven-Göran Eriksson in 2000 he was lauded for his calmness and restraint – yet two years later when England slumped to defeat by Brazil in the World Cup, the same 'cool' Swede was criticised for lacking the blood-and-thunder approach we were supposed to have rejected. Now the new king of cool had lost his crown. Mourinho's honeymoon was over.

Some people thought the 'Shush' gesture innocuous, arguing that if Liverpool fans could not cope with a bit of banter they were in the wrong game. Others thought it ridiculously childish behaviour for someone in a position of leadership. Certainly if a player had done anything exceptionally silly – if Wayne Rooney had scored for Manchester United on his return to Everton, say, then mooned at the crowd and been sent off – he could have expected condemnation on all sides. And, had the hypothetical offender been a Chelsea player, he would surely have been referred to the strict code of conduct every squad member was handed after Mourinho arrived at Stamford Bridge. Later Mourinho was to touch on the issue of what was and was not acceptable, saying he had seen Adriano celebrate with such a gesture after scoring a goal for Inter without upsetting anyone. It was not the first time he had used Adriano to illustrate a point. Nor was it the first time Mourinho had confused himself with a star footballer. But there is a difference, surely, between the standards expected of a coach and a player, just as the teacher is expected to be above the more mischievous traits of the pupil. Critics wondered if such debates might be raging within a polyglot squad. But word came back that the dressing room was solidly behind Mourinho the winner. So the players did not see him as a posturing narcissist.

In the pre-Mourinho period, a prevalent characteristic of top coaches in England was the knack of being able to mask any selfishness in their ambition. Sir Alex Ferguson always gave the impression of being willing to fight for his players if necessary, Arsène Wenger of regarding them almost as his own flesh and blood. Mourinho infuses the players with his own super-confidence, creating an almost evangelical atmosphere. In this sense, he follows in the tradition of Bill Shankly, who made Liverpool's Anfield stadium a fortress in the sixties. Once, when an inexperienced reporter for the *Guardian* in Manchester, I resolved to interview Shankly by phone. The subject my sports editor had chosen was Ian Callaghan, a midfielder for whom Shankly had an acknowledged and understandable affection. I rang Anfield and asked to be put through to Shankly – these days you would be transferred to a media department which would advise you to come to the manager's weekly briefing or, if that were too late for your purpose, consult the club's website – and the next thing I knew a familiar rasping voice, the sort of voice you would get by crossing James Cagney with a Scottish coal miner, was on the line.

'Yes!'

He had to say it twice because I hesitated, feeling not only unworthy but, to be honest, frightened.

'Mr Shankly?'

'Yes! Yes!'

'Um, Mr Shankly, what do you think of Ian Callaghan?'

There was a silence that seemed to last an eternity before Shankly spoke again. And then he spat it out:

'Jesus Christ!'

I was about to apologise for having troubled him when he continued: 'Aye, son, Jesus Christ.' And I realised he was answering my question. 'Cally's the nearest thing on this earth to Jesus Christ.' The way he lived his life was an example to all; he was gentle and yet courageous; and so it went on, Shankly talking vividly while my heart pounded at the excitement of securing such a dramatic tribute as the introduction to my piece. Shankly had a similar level of admiration for quite a few of his players, among them Kevin Keegan and the late Emlyn Hughes, and never hesitated to express it and, partly in consequence, they felt and behaved like worldbeaters.

There was a reminder of this when Mourinho spoke before the trip to Barcelona. In truth, for all Sir Alex Ferguson might have been saying about luck, Chelsea had not been enjoying the best of it. In particular they had lost Arjen Robben through injury – not for the first time and not for the last during a season in which the young Dutchman still demonstrated that, if allowed more opportunities to shine, he might have beaten even Frank Lampard and John Terry to the player-of-the-year awards. Robben had been the victim of a fearsome tackle by Aaron Mokoena at Blackburn and a journalist wondered if Mourinho now wished he had bought a reinforcement in the wide-attacker department during the winter transfer window that had just closed – if only as a temporary measure. Mourinho had stayed out of the market. Was that not taking a risk? Mourinho answered scornfully. 'If I had bought someone for that position,' he said, '*that* would have been a big risk. Because the player I bought could have been on the bench for months. To replace Duff and Robben – no chance! You could buy one of the best players in the world – and he'd end up having to sit on the bench.' It did not answer the question but, as endorsements go, it didn't half ring.

Then Mourinho was asked about his young captain, John Terry, who was having such an inspirational season in the Premiership as to be a hot tip for at least one of the awards (in the event Terry was chosen by the players while Lampard won the football writers' vote). English football was one thing, though, Europe quite another and Barcelona had candidates for world awards. Surely, the next questioner suggested, an attack featuring Ronaldinho and Samuel Eto'o would present a big test of Terry's progress. 'It will be a big test,' replied Mourinho, 'for them.'

Can you imagine how Terry and his team-mates felt when they read their papers the next morning?

Just a few weeks later, however, in the aftermath of their aggregate victory over Bayern Munich in the next

round, Mourinho was actually being accused of oversha-
dowing his players' achievements. Under UEFA rules
governing the suspension of coaches, he had been banned
from having any contact with his players after they
arrived at the stadium for each leg. There were the
earpiece antics at Stamford Bridge, where he was
suspected of transmitting messages by way of a device
concealed in the woolly hat of his fitness coach, Rui Faria,
and the sudden exit from the stands at Munich's Olympic
Stadium when he felt he was being crowded by
photographers, journalists and German fans and fled by
taxi to the team hotel to watch the match on television.
Every day, it seemed, there was a fresh vignette, a new
controversy, another reason for Mourinho to hog the
headlines. 'I'm not interested in myself,' he insisted. 'I'm
not interested in my image and what people think about
me, only in getting results. Some of the things I say and
do, I'm just thinking of the group. They know me. They
understand that.' The players certainly seemed to; they
queued to attest that, far from Mourinho's behaviour
being a distraction from the pursuit of the biggest prizes,
it actually helped them by lightening the pressure.
Meanwhile the method in the apparent madness of his
tilting at the UEFA windmill was to make the team feel
somehow threatened, cornered and required to stand
together against any danger that ensued. To induce the
underdog spirit in probably the most financially potent
football club the world has ever seen is quite an

achievement, but Mourinho's Chelsea never got too comfortable, never went soft, until the battle they most wanted to win, that for the Premiership title, was won.

The enemy of football

Far from being chastened by the widespread revulsion at his comments about the referee in Barcelona, Mourinho told the Portuguese media within a matter of days that the result had been 'adulterated' owing to Frisk's dismissal of Drogba. He was called to account by an irate UEFA and later, after a thrilling Chelsea victory on aggregate at Stamford Bridge had culminated in further rancour – this time the crucial refereeing decision went Mourinho's way as Pierluigi Collina ignored Barcelona's protests that Ricardo Carvalho had illicitly prevented their goalkeeper, Victor Valdés, from reaching John Terry's winning header – Mourinho was ordered to sit out the quarter-final. Coach and club were also fined for the relatively technical offences of having snubbed the press and neglected, despite exhortations, to get their team on the Barcelona pitch in time for the second half to start on schedule. Stevie Clarke, one of his assistants, and a security officer, Les Miles, were admonished by UEFA for their parts in the formation of the tale about Rijkaard's visit to the referee's room; Mourinho had since admitted he had seen nothing and relied on the testimony of the pair, whom UEFA deemed guilty of a mere misunderstanding caused by the layout of the stadium.

This is how Mourinho's story lurched ungraciously towards the inevitable, in his own words:

At first: *'When I saw Rijkaard entering the referee's dressing room I couldn't believe it. When Didier Drogba was sent off I wasn't surprised.'*

Several days later: *'Rijkaard was in the referee's room for over five minutes. I know because my assistants were at the door while the meeting took place.'*

And finally, after he had taken refuge in legal advice to go easy on the subject for a while: *'If something happens in a football stadium, and I don't see it, and if some of my people say to me, "I saw this, this happened," and if another one arrives and says, "It's true," I have to believe my people. I have to treat it as the truth, use it as the truth. Because I cannot work without loyalty. I have to believe my people. So, because I'm loyal to my people, I'm involved in something I don't want.'*

Chelsea had been outraged by statements from William Gaillard, UEFA's head of communications, who had accused them of, among other things, 'using lies as a pre-match tactic ahead of the second leg' with Barcelona. Who can say whether those falsehoods affected Collina's performance? Certainly there were no lingering complaints from Barcelona. But they were out of the Champions League and Mourinho was in disgrace, offering coded explanations to which no one was really listening.

Meanwhile it had become clear that the real victim of the episode would be an innocent party. Frisk had suddenly retired from refereeing at forty-two (the same age as Mourinho), saying he was 'scared to let my children leave the house' after threats received by post, telephone and email. The Swede, a little too demonstrative in style and blond-streaked in appearance for some tastes but officially rated behind only Collina in the world, rejected appeals to reconsider from, among others, the chairman of the UEFA referees' committee, Volker Roth, who expressed his revulsion by declaring: 'People like Mourinho are the enemy of football.' Roth was right in the sense that coaches who casually make the referee's lot more onerous and stressful are sabotaging the chances of good decisions; Frisk did say the reason he was leaving the game was that he could no longer trust himself, by which he clearly meant guarantee the purity of his decision-making. But mostly there was just basic human sympathy for him. As the Swiss referee Urs Meier, who had been a victim of similarly vile English threats after denying Sven-Göran Eriksson's national team a goal against Portugal in the European Championship eight months earlier, put it, rather mildly: 'UEFA and FIFA [the world body] have to protect referees from attacks like this.'

A certain disaffection with Chelsea had set in. They were portrayed as an arrogant, bullying club with *nouveau riche* values. Arsène Wenger made a fair point when he asked why Abramovich did not come out and show some leadership – 'I'd like to hear a voice at Chelsea say what they really want to do, what they want to be in England and how they want to behave' – but there was no response and so Mourinho continued to take most of the criticism. The newspapers gave it, energetically and, at times, hysterically, publishing lists of supposed misdemeanours that soon became risible, with anything remotely connected with a difference of opinion being laid at Mourinho's door. One supposed diary of disgrace actually began:

Sept 12, 2004: *Accuses referee Rob Styles of being 'ridiculous' after he fails to give Didier Drogba a penalty in the 0–0 draw at Aston Villa.*

Well, well. A coach is not enamoured of a referee's judgement. Whatever next? In fact, television had proved Mourinho right. But the list went on.

Sept 29: *Is spat at by Porto fan before Chelsea's 3–1 win at Stamford Bridge in the Champions League.*

Mourinho's part in this crime – provoking the fan by his presence, perhaps – was not described. Nor was it explained why the next charge on the sheet, that of being accused by Adrian Mutu of lying during the Romanian forward's period of serious cocaine abuse, had stuck.

Coincidentally a couple of charges were brought by the FA which must have vexed Mourinho. First Chelsea were fined £15,000 for 'failing to control their players' at Blackburn, where the home side's robust approach had cost Chelsea the services of Arjen Robben. Then Mourinho himself was relieved of £5,000 for having observed of Manchester United's performance in a Carling Cup semi-final: 'In the second half it was whistle and whistle and whistle, fault and fault, cheat and cheat.' The FA should have known Mourinho was not really calling United cheats. When using the word 'fault', by which he meant 'foul', in conjunction with 'cheat', he was talking about tactical fouling, which, whether we like it or not, is part of the game and should be a legitimate subject of discussion. No wonder, after all the fuss Celtic and Manchester United had made about Porto's little tricks, he was angry about these fines. But he was getting to know our ways and the finer nuances of our footballing vocabulary: to refer to an opponent's 'cheating' had become politically incorrect. Except, of course, in relation to foreigners (defined as non-English players who make their living outside the Premiership) such as Deco.

The Frisk affair was more significant in any language, and although, as Chelsea went into the last month of the season, Mourinho admitted he had made mistakes – 'it is not necessary to fight every day' – he continued to betray no hint of sympathy for the referee. He even made a joke about Frisk on Portuguese television that verged on the callous. Asked to comment on Porto's 2–0 defeat by Sporting Lisbon, during which his former club had had two players sent off, Mourinho smiled and replied: 'I have to be very careful when I talk about referees because Mr João Ferreira may also quit refereeing.' Clearly Frisk's retirement was not weighing too heavily on his conscience.

It was, then, very much in a spirit of defiance that Mourinho approached the visit of Bayern to Stamford Bridge. He even took the opportunity to play mind games with his own employers and Chelsea's first weekend of April, though it included a victory at Southampton, was utterly dominated by reports of how Kenyon and, of course, Abramovich had been made aware that he was (a) not very happy with the standard of support the club had given him during the rows with UEFA, who had themselves privately complained about the attitude of at least one Chelsea employee involved, and (b) not wholly against the notion of a contract extension on highly favourable terms. The contract question had been under discussion for some time but Mourinho's standing had become so high that he only had to cough for everyone at Chelsea to catch a cold – everyone, but everyone – and so at Peter Kenyon's suggestion Abramovich flew in to meet Mourinho and his agent, Jorge Mendes. Suddenly all was sweetness and light and the only argument to be heard was between journalists on the question of how much Mourinho's next contract would be worth. A basic £5.2 million a year – a rise of £1 million, presumably – was the lowest estimate. The highest was £9 million, including bonuses and image rights.

Mourinho watched his team beat Bayern 4–2 on television in the fitness centre of the Chelsea Village Hotel, less than 100 yards from the pitch, and throughout the match events on the bench engaged the media almost as frequently as the excellence of Frank Lampard, who scored one very good goal and one, featuring a chest-trap, turn and half-volley, all in the same smooth movement, that was quite sumptuous, of balletic elegance. Meanwhile Rui Faria, the fitness coach, kept fiddling with the area around his right ear, inducing a suspicion that Mourinho was passing messages to his assistants by telephone, as he had boasted of doing when with Porto. Every now and again a note would be scribbled and handed to Clarke or Mourinho's most senior assistant, Baltemar Brito. Once again Chelsea's players were struggling for space on the back pages the next morning – against their own manager, who had not even been in the stadium. It was becoming more and more difficult to accept what he had said after Cardiff: 'I'm not interested in my image . . . I'm just thinking of the group. They know me, they understand that.'

It ought to be added, in fairness to Mourinho, that the

antics of his sidekicks were clearly for the benefit of the players rather than the media. Anyway, insisted Rui Faria, when he turned up in Munich as Mourinho's spokesman at the pre-match press conference: 'I did not have anything under my hat last week and people worry about too many silly things.' Just to be sure, UEFA officials went to him at half-time and ordered him to remove his hat; nothing was found. As an example of closing the stable door after the horse had bolted, this was unbeatable. Chelsea came through the match more comfortably than the 6–5 aggregate score might suggest, earning a semi-final against Liverpool which, given the mutual respect between Mourinho and his counterpart Rafael Benítez, was bound to pulsate in a vigorous but relatively civilised and adult manner.

Liverpool's supporters played their part. Shortly before the first leg at Stamford Bridge, a scoreless stalemate, Mourinho left his players and staff in the dressing room and strode deep in thought to the bench to sit alone, as is his custom. He may have forgotten that the area next to the bench at Chelsea is allocated to visiting fans. At any rate, he was soon approached by several Liverpudlians making 'Shush' gestures. Mourinho, grinning broadly, gave them the thumbs-up before posing for a mobile-phone photograph.

The match was played in a similar spirit and at the end of a deafening second leg, decided in Liverpool's favour by the decision of the Slovakian referee Luboš Michel to award a goal to Luis García in the opening minutes, Mourinho paid tribute to the crowd's influence. There was a double edge to his remarks, for he went on to claim that William Gallas had cleared the ball before the whole of it had crossed the line and blamed one of Michel's linesmen, Roman Slyško, for having signalled a goal; the official, he implied, had been swayed by the Anfield atmosphere. While a body of opinion, fortified by Sky computer images, sympathised with him on this, others pointed out that, if Michel and Slyško had been of a mind to apply the letter of the law rigorously against Chelsea, the referee could have given a penalty against Petr Čech, who had bowled over Milan Baroš seconds earlier, and shown the goalkeeper the red card, leaving Mourinho's team with ten men for almost the whole match.

Anyway, Liverpool and their fevered supporters deserved to reach a final they were destined to win dramatically, even if Mourinho, in asserting afterwards that the better team had lost on this occasion, was unable to resist the temptation to allude to the truth as demonstrated by the Premiership League table.

Chelsea went very close to punching their weight. In the sixth and last minute of time added for stoppages, Eidur Gudjohnsen put wide the sort of chance you would expect him to take. But if Chelsea had prevailed it would have been nothing to do with Mourinho's powers, to which Liverpool, under the more restrained but undoubtedly crafty Benítez, seemed impervious. While spectators, their veins bulging, roared and screamed, the technical area marked out in front of the dugouts staged an oddly dignified play within a play. At one stage Benítez and Mourinho, coincidentally running out to the boundary line to signal instructions to their players, bumped into each other; each briefly smiled, half-turned inwards and raised his arms in a symmetrical gesture of apology. Towards the end of the match, Mourinho became a still, small figure who had run out of ideas and accepted tactical defeat; he had thrown on the beefy young German defender Robert Huth as an additional striker, a ploy hardly calculated to furrow the brows of Sami Hyypia and the outstanding Jamie Carragher. After the final whistle, he went to his players. There were hugs for Terry and Lampard and a special squeeze for the freshly frustrated Gudjohnsen, and then handshakes for the jubilant Liverpool side were followed by applause for the crowd from Mourinho as he disappeared down the tunnel.

Would he now shush? A likely scenario. His complaints about Slyško were made without any reference to the decisions that had worked in his teams' favour when Porto survived at Manchester United the previous season and Chelsea triumphed over Barcelona; selective myopia is a widespread affliction among coaches. Whether he chose his words carefully only he can know, but he stopped short of inviting a UEFA charge before, for some reason, reiterating his belief in God and promising that his planning for the next season would start right away.

The principal objective for the current season had been attained only seventy-three hours earlier – Mourinho was still complaining that the Premiership fixture schedule worked against Chelsea's interests in Europe – when they secured the English title at Bolton, two goals from Frank Lampard causing a limited celebration. When Mourinho spotted the players taking an odd swig from the champagne bottles they had been using to spray each other, he 'got the hump' according to a grinning Lampard, and told them to remember Anfield. But he was as happy and fulfilled as anyone else. A few weeks earlier, Mourinho had vouchsafed: 'I predicted at the start of the season that we would win the title in April.' It was April 30 and Mourinho's men were hugging each other. To quote the slogan more precisely: he had done *exactly* what it said on the tin.

The work still to be done meant he could not keep a pledge to stand back once the title was safe, 'to disappear a little bit and let the players enjoy themselves and be the face of our success'. Some hope! The day after Chelsea took the title, a BBC website offering the public 'shares' in sports personalities priced in accordance with the newspaper column inches devoted to them – Mourinho had for some months been the most expensive – showed him at £132.04. You could have Lampard at £16.54 and

Terry at £10.77. Wayne Rooney shares were the second priciest at £22.58. So the option of relative obscurity was not open to Mourinho. But, in brief deference to his promise, he was more restrained at Bolton than on other occasions and an indelible image of that warm evening at the Reebok Stadium is of him alone in the dugout with his mobile phone and the loveliest, most relaxed smile, one that exuded pure pleasure rather than the triumphalism normally evident on these occasions. When he had finished, the Sky interviewer Geoff Shreeves went over and asked who the conversation had been with and he replied: 'My wife, my kids.' It was difficult to believe that this was the belligerent blusterer of Barcelona, the carping curmudgeon of Cardiff, but they were all one and the same. We had before us a much more complicated character than Mourinho's initial conquest of the English game's affections may have suggested.

When I asked Sir Bobby Robson if Mourinho had rubbed people up the wrong way in Portugal or Spain as he had done since coming to England, he answered: 'No, never. Not in our time together anyway.' So he, Robson, had never seen the strutting figure who taunted the Liverpool supporters in Cardiff? 'No, not really.' So what had changed him – fame? 'Well,' said Robson, 'let me tell you. And it's happened to me. It happens to all of us. We acquire a bit of power, don't we? Through success. You get a bit of power. You know what you stand for. You know what people think of you. And this power, this control you have over people, becomes ingrained into you. You develop a stronger personality. Look at Brian Clough and the way he developed. At one time Cloughie wasn't the Old Big 'Ead he became. He always had visions that he might get that way, probably, but he had to behave in a certain manner. All successful managers, if you look at them, have that strength of personality. You use your position to be powerful. More powerful than you basically are.'

The notion of Mourinho as a victim of the syndrome, a managerial megalomaniac, is seductive; after all, he became accustomed to dominance at Porto, and now he has the purse of one of the world's richest men with which to build an empire. But Robson's great friend Gérard Houllier thought the motivation was more likely to be a desire for revenge than power. 'I can imagine he'd had a lot of abuse at the Millennium Stadium,' the Lyon and former Liverpool coach continued, 'because Chelsea had been 1–0 down for a long time. So he was saying to them, "You've had a go at me – now be quiet." Like players do.' But he is not a player and the difference was outlined by William Gaillard, the UEFA official who so irked Chelsea when he accepted that Mourinho had not intended to whip up such serious malice as Anders Frisk was made to suffer but added: 'Coaches are role models for players and fans. They have a duty to behave better than anyone else.' Was that not the case? Houllier nodded. So had Mourinho not gone too far in Barcelona?

'Yes, but it's easy to say that sitting in a comfortable chair in a quiet room when there's no crowd in your ears and things going on. In our job, we sometimes get a bit paranoid.'

Quite so. And when I told Houllier what I have seen it do to the most civilised and intelligent of them – notably induce the emission of utter twaddle, especially on the subject of referees – he gave a chuckle of recognition. 'I know – even Arsène!' Neither Wenger nor Houllier has been known to tell a crowd to shut up. But Wenger on occasion has defended the indefensible and Houllier seethed against referees. 'I think,' said Houllier, 'that, when things don't go your way, you are trying to rationalise, to find an explanation, and sometimes that leads you down the wrong road. Now I have gone back into management I hope I'll be different, because I've been on the other side, working for French television, and can see the futility of how we sometimes behave. It's incredible. I never saw it before. I can see now that even José Mourinho gives too much importance to certain things. But in his place, a few years ago, I'd have felt no differently. And what we have to remember is that, despite the brilliance of José's career, he is still in the early stages of it. And the more he wins the more humble he will get. Let's put it this way: he's a rough diamond who will gradually become smoother and better, both as a coach and as a man.'

That may or may not happen. It happened with Brian

Clough, who, though alcoholism began to sap his strength when he was not much older than Mourinho is now, became one of the most principled of managers; when Clough died, past referees lined up to form a metaphorical guard of honour, for his teams had been models of discipline. Whether Mourinho will ever bring to his manipulative skills such an unashamedly moral dimension remains to be seen. Yet during a break in Chelsea's season there was evidence that he valued things other than the pursuit of victory. At the end of March, when his players dispersed to join their various national squads for World Cup qualifying matches, Mourinho flew to Israel. He had been approached two months earlier by the Peres Center for Peace and asked for help in drawing worldwide attention to a programme designed to foster peace by bringing together Israeli and Palestinian children to play football in mixed teams. Mourinho readily agreed and the commitment he displayed during a three-day visit impressed every observer. With Shimon Peres, the deputy prime minister, he mingled with countless children and one day he gave a lecture to around 250 Israeli and Palestinian coaches, complete with visual projections he had clearly taken the trouble to prepare himself, drawing on experience; Mourinho was a teacher for three years before he went into football full-time. The odd instance of semantic originality – 'improvisibility' was one concept that lost something in translation – only added to the charm. Even hard-to-impress journalists were enthralled. 'When it was over,' one told me, 'I looked at my watch and he'd been speaking for an hour and thirty-five minutes. The time had flashed by.'

Another writer who went on the trip, Matt Hughes of the London *Evening Standard*, wrote that, when Mourinho stood back in his white T-shirt to address an enlarged photograph of himself and Frank Lampard locked in an embrace after the Carling Cup final, he went all sensitive, as if sharing his wedding pictures with the audience. 'This,' Mourinho told the coaches, 'looks like a hug, but it's more than a hug . . . this is a hug that shows we trust each other. Without words he's saying to me "Thanks" and I'm saying to him "Thanks". This is a hug that we repeat player after player because we are a family.' Upon reading that, I thought about Adrian Mutu, the player thrown out of the Chelsea family for taking cocaine. Then I reflected that there can be a limit to any parent's patience. It is natural, sometimes, when you listen to the puffed-up figures of a coach's speech, to think: bullshit. But Mutu, like every player on the Chelsea staff at the start of the 2004–05 season, was told Mourinho wanted only players willing to gear everything, including their social lives, to the demands of success. The Romanian broke his implicit promise and, after ignoring warnings, had to be punished for it. But at the end of every moral discussion surrounding Mourinho you came back to the same question: what had the family of Anders Frisk done to offend him? Football, for all the light it might occasionally bring into the lives of the children of the Gaza Strip, can be a nasty business.

Mourinho, according to Chelsea's *bête noire*, William Gaillard of UEFA, had brought 'a lot of new things to football, many of them positive', but he had to remember he was in a position of responsibility. The trouble with being a top-level coach, however, is that it involves such a lot of acting. And how can a man be sure what his position is when briefly – in the interests of the team, of course – he has forgotten who *he* is. Coaches are often ham actors, playing to the gallery or the media, sometimes with a different act for each. José Mourinho is unusual; he is like a one-man show in which he plays a wide variety of roles. He can do a passable megalomaniac, or be paranoid. He can strut in full of bombast, nakedly adversarial, ready to take on the world. Or he can be vulnerable; often, when he is in this frame of mind, a shark metaphor is just around the corner (understandably enough, given that he was brought up so near the Portuguese coast). At the height of his conflict with UEFA and Barcelona, he mused: 'I feel like a boy swimming between sharks.' When there is a lull, you come to expect a storm, and the other way round. And yet he always seems to surprise us, to hold our attention and keep us guessing, just as those of a certain age will remember Clough being able to. There have been articles in the broadsheets discussing the connection between madness and genius (or at least eccentricity and being an outstanding football manager) which you could well have imagined adorning the colour supplements in Clough's day. Clough liked to swing from mood to mood. He would portray himself as a dictator one day, a caring socialist the next – in 1973 he was described by Malcolm Allison, another of the more flamboyant managers, as 'a kind of Rolls-Royce communist'.

Most managers have tended to specialise in a certain kind of role. George Graham, who guided Arsenal to the English championship in 1989 and 1991, was always pleased to be considered a strict disciplinarian. He played up to it and, even though there was usually a slight twinkle in his eye, it was seldom noticed. Yet during his time in charge the club's disciplinary record off the field left a lot to be desired. Tony Adams, before he began his inspiring recovery from alcoholism, even served a term of imprisonment for a driving offence which could only be described as extreme. As for Arsenal's on-the-field repute, suffice it to say that in the glorious season of 1990–91, when they lost but a single match in the League (to Chelsea), the only other people to take more than a point out of a meeting with them were the FA, who docked two as a punishment for their part in a twenty-one-man brawl at Old Trafford (Alex Ferguson's Manchester United had one point deducted). There was one very disciplined aspect of Graham's Arsenal: the defence. So maybe he will always be reviewed in the stern image of his back four. Nor will Graham – in real life, always one of the most pleasant and approachable men in the managerial game – mind going down in history as, if not quite football's answer to Captain Bligh of the *Bounty*, a man who liked nothing more than to run a tight ship.

I sometimes think these people are having fun at our expense; I really do. There was often a whimsical air about Clough that suggested he could see through football and the people in it. Maybe one day Mourinho will reach that stage. But for now he is very different, all but admitting he can tailor his mood to suit what he judges to be his team's requirements at any given time. It is, however, surely fair to scrutinise the theory that, as he put it eight days before the Premiership title was claimed: 'While I have been fighting every day, there has been calm around the team.' Does it actually calm a player when his boss is marched down the Millennium Stadium tunnel with half an hour of a cup final to go and the score 1–1? If that were a sight guaranteed to improve a team's performance, every coach would be trying to get himself collared. True, the vast montage of newspaper headlines that turned nine months of Mourinho's professional life into the first series of a soap opera must have lightened the mood at Chelsea's training ground, where everyone exuded confidence in the knowledge that they could tell where the act ended and Mourinho their friend and leader began. Mourinho alluded to this when, on the eve of the Champions League visit to Anfield, he said: 'I'm not selfish. I'm not the man some people think I am.

Only the players really know what and who I am.' But, for the rest of us, the task of working out a little of Mourinho and analysing why he chooses to do things in the way he does is tricky.

He is an exceptionally gifted psychologist – that much is clear – and a great deal besides. Which is what they used to say about Carl Gustav Jung, the original differentiator between extrovert and introvert personalities. My wild guess would be that Mourinho is an extrovert. But, if we are to discover a bit more, we might as well begin, as the real analysts do, with the child.

PART TWO

The formative years

Born into football

On 26 January 1963, John F. Kennedy was President of the United States. He had less than a year to live; it was the 700th of his 1,000 days. Harold Macmillan was Britain's Prime Minister and that morning he would have noted the West German cabinet's unanimous declaration of support for British entry into the Common Market, which was to grow into the European Union. The notion of Portuguese membership of the Common Market would have been almost laughable because, quite apart from its relative poverty, Portugal had been a dictatorship since 1926. Although outwardly tranquil enough, it still harboured a widespread fear of António Salazar's political police, the Polícia Internacional de Defesa do Estado, or PIDE. So much for the political situation. Now for the sport and weather. So deep was this British midwinter that all but eight ties in the fourth round of the FA Cup were postponed and Chelsea flew to Malta to escape the freeze. On 26 January, they played a local select team in Valletta. Meanwhile in Portugal the game went on, dominated by the Benfica of Eusébio, Mário Coluna and José Águas, who had been champions of Europe in each of the previous two seasons (and were to reach the final again that year, only to lose to Milan at Wembley). Benfica were not only respected throughout Europe for their marvellously skilful football but considered rather exotic because, unusually among European sides at that time, they had black players. They had come from the African colonies: Eusébio and Coluna were from Mozambique, Joaquim Santana from Angola. On 26 January, the great Eusébio and his team-mates were engaged in the recovery of the national title from their Lisbon rivals Sporting (they were to win it by a substantial margin). And in the port of Setúbal, just twenty miles south of Lisbon, where the Sado river joins the Atlantic, the creature eventually to be known throughout the world as José Mourinho was born.

His full name was José Mário dos Santos Mourinho Félix. His father was Félix Mourinho, a professional footballer, a goalkeeper who was to represent Portugal, albeit only once and very, very briefly. Indeed so short was Félix Mourinho's international career to be that, if you had put an egg on to boil as it started, you would only just have turned off the gas, spooned the egg from the pan and cracked the thing open when it ended. It lasted from the eighty-second minute of a match against the Republic of Ireland in Recife, Brazil, until the final whistle. Yes, Félix Mourinho had a mere eight minutes in his country's service, as a substitute for José Henrique. At least he kept a clean sheet. Portugal were leading the Irish 2–1 when he came on and it stayed that way.

You may wonder what the Portuguese and Irish squads were doing on the north-east coast of Brazil. They had been invited by the host nation to take part in a tournament called the Independence Cup in the summer of 1972. Brazil won it, beating Portugal 1–0 in the final, which was no surprise because two years earlier the Brazilians had lifted the World Cup by the abundant virtue of a team some judges still consider the finest in football's entire history: Pelé, Jairzinho, Rivelino and Gérson were among its stars. Portugal's star of stars, Eusébio, could probably have done without the Independence Cup. He was over thirty and years of brutal tackling had taken a toll of his legs. 'I was instructed to do a man-to-man marking job on him,' recalls Ireland's Mick Martin, later to begin a career in England with Manchester United but at that time a spindly twenty-one-year-old part-timer running a Dublin sports shop, 'and I felt I kept the great man pretty quiet. I'm serious – our manager, Liam Tuohy, told me that too.' Félix Mourinho, like Mick Martin, would always remember 25 June 1972. But first he would go home and tell his family about it. Especially his son. His nine-year-old son José.

Félix Mourinho had long been acknowledged in

Portugal as a proficient last line of defence and had made a more than respectable career with both Vitória of Setúbal and later Lisbon's third force after Benfica and Sporting, Belenenses, for whom he was playing at the age of thirty-five when he went to the tournament in Brazil.

Young José and his sister Teresa, four years his elder, had a comfortable start in life. They grew up among an extended family in a large house on the estate of their wealthy great-uncle, Mário Ascensão Ledo, the owner of sardine canneries in not only Setúbal but Oporto and the Algarve, whose beneficence had included the donation of land and money for the building of the Vitória club's Bonfim Stadium. Both materially and emotionally, José was well looked after. He attended a private school and, when he came home, there were trees to provide shade in the garden, where he played football, sometimes with his father and sometimes with one of the family's servants, an elderly man; in addition there were two maids. His father also took him horse-riding. 'Although José was always small,' an aunt said, 'he had no fear.' But most of his spare moments were devoted to football. Either playing or watching his father train; Félix loved to take José to work and clearly intended to give the boy every chance of following in his footsteps to the professional ranks. José's mother, Maria Júlia Mourinho (née Ledo), was a primary-school teacher whose spare time would often be spent on church activities. A devout Catholic with a strong personality, she made sure José attended to matters spiritual; he was to remain religious in adulthood, sometimes visiting the shrine at Fátima, a couple of hours' drive to the north of Lisbon.

In 1974, by which time the power of Portuguese football had receded to the extent that Benfica were knocked out of Europe in the early rounds in consecutive seasons – by Derby County and the Hungarian club Újpest Dózsa – José was eleven and something truly significant happened around him. He lived through a revolution. He may not have noticed, because it was a very Portuguese handover of power, a near-bloodless triumph for the forces of democracy, which, to the advantage of José's generation as a whole and José in particular, made educational improvements a high priority. There is a certain irony here. The family benefactor, Mário Ascensão Ledo, had prospered under the old authoritarian regime, the fall of which was followed by a great wave of educational advancement, which José rode. By now Ledo was dead and the canneries had been lost to the revolution – or, as the aunt put it, 'taken by the communists' – but modern Portugal was to serve at least one member of the family well. It is doubtful that José Mourinho would have made a living in football without the key that his academic accomplishments, above all his excellence at languages, were to constitute. For he was never quite good enough at playing to live up to the fond hopes he and his father had entertained. He was no more than what the English used to call a decent amateur.

In 1974, José had still to realise that. He clung to his dreams. Like most adolescents, he cherished his heroes too, and one was Kevin Keegan, who inspired Liverpool's emphatic victory over Newcastle in that year's FA Cup final at Wembley. José supported Liverpool from afar and, when Keegan left for Hamburg in 1977, passed his affections on to Keegan's replacement, Kenny Dalglish; he was also an admirer of Graeme Souness. Those able to cast their minds back to the days when the Scots Dalglish and Souness (with stylish assistance from their compatriot Alan Hansen) were driving Liverpool to supremacy in Europe may have an image of Souness fashioning for Dalglish the goal against Bruges at Wembley that meant the club retained the European title in 1978. It was around that time when reality dawned on Mourinho and he began the process of acceptance that he would never be a top professional footballer. Later, talking it over with his father, he announced that he would instead strive to become the best coach in the world. And Félix, who had himself become a coach after hanging up his goalkeeper's gloves, liked the sound of that, because he already knew his son had a talent for reading the game.

He had encouraged it by giving José tasks to perform for his clubs: early in Félix's coaching career, at Caldas, a little third-division club, he sent José to write assessments of rival teams. As Félix made a growing impact, moving to the second-division Amora, near Setúbal, and supervising a successful campaign for promotion to the first division in 1978–79, José also began to learn tricks of the trade: Félix would put him in charge of the ball-boys and have him send messages to players during matches. Coaching came naturally to José and within a few years, having left university, he was looking after Vitória Setúbal's Under-16s.

It was nevertheless important for him to play while he could. Mourinho was a defender. An occasional central midfielder too. But basically a central defender. You may think it odd that, having grown up in the era of Eusébio, an attacker so dynamic and thrilling some judges considered him superior to Pelé, a boy would choose to play at the relatively unglamorous back end of the team. But someone has to defend and José Mourinho, though not physically built in such a way as to suggest he would be a natural bulwark of the rearguard, enjoyed the opportunity that position gave him to organise his colleagues and the game. He is remembered as skilful but not over-endowed with speed or the fighting spirit later to be exemplified by his Chelsea captain, John Terry. Nor was he especially keen on the tireless running coaches crave: a trait later noticeable when, during his widely publicised visit to the Peres Center in Tel Aviv, the Chelsea coach took a somewhat languid part in an informal match. So José Mourinho had a modest playing career, which he combined with school and, after an unscheduled gap year, university studies.

It began in the youth section at Belenenses, where his

father's playing career had finished. Then, when Félix became coach at Rio Ave up in the north, beyond Oporto, he engaged his eighteen-year-old son as a player for one season. Quite a season it was too: Rio Ave finished fifth in the first division, their highest position ever. But José was not able to live at that level. He never got beyond the reserves. He did, however, nearly make it to the first team on the last day of that season. Rio Ave were about to take on Sporting, who needed to win to be sure of the championship, in the Alvalade Stadium in Lisbon when one of their defenders was injured during the warm-up. Félix told his son to get changed. To this day José Mourinho dislikes being reminded that the club president, José Maria Pinho, countermanded Félix's order. All he has said is that, because his father was in a difficult position, his appearances were restricted. At Rio Ave there is no record of his having worn the shirt at all. At any rate, José could hardly have made things worse that day at the Alvalade: Sporting won 7–0. Father and son returned to their roots and José, upon entering university in Lisbon, played for the reserves at Belenenses, where his father had a second-division season. José went on to have spells with minor clubs in the Setúbal area. And that was about it.

He was a good scholar – all secondary-school pupils in Portugal must learn at least two languages, and Mourinho had no difficulties with that – but not universally brilliant. In fact poor marks at mathematics disqualified him from entering university at the first attempt. Hence the year up north. He continued his maths studies during that time with his father and repeated the examination before starting at the Instituto Superior de Educação Física in Lisbon. There, his gift for languages (he could speak English, French, Spanish and Italian, and several years later, when he went to Barcelona with Bobby Robson, Catalan players and staff were to appreciate his taking the trouble to acquire a grasp of the regional tongue) allowed him to read widely on the physiology and psychology of sporting achievement. He listened intently to the philosophy lectures of Manuel Sérgio, from whom Mourinho began to derive a fascination for playing with people's emotions. The professor remembers him as a voracious student: 'He looked like a cat catching birds.'

After obtaining a degree in sports science, Mourinho taught PE for three years at junior and secondary schools in and around Setúbal – Arangues, Alhos Vedros and Bela Vista – and helped handicapped children to learn sports. One of his former pupils at Arangues, André Chin, recalls Mourinho with warmth: 'He was a very good teacher, very comprehensive in his approach, interested in all the kids. If you had a problem, you could go to him with it. Everybody got along with him. Football was always his big thing. He coached some friends of mine at Vitória Setúbal, youngsters of fourteen or fifteen, and there was one particular kid he thought had potential and tried to

help, a black kid called António who went on to play for
the Portuguese national youth team. I still see António
from time to time. He's a salesman for cable TV. He
didn't make it as a player.' This may have been connected
with an incident in which António got drunk, overslept,
missed training and was hauled out of bed by Mourinho,
who told him he could forget joining the rest of the lads
on a forthcoming trip to a tournament in France. Or, as
André Chin decorously put it: 'I don't think António had
quite enough desire or dedication to become a professional footballer.'

It was always like this in the field of youth development: even the most gifted need an inner drive. By now
Mourinho's own ambition was focused on coaching. In
1988 he spent a week of his summer break from teaching
in Scotland, obtaining the first part of his UEFA coaching
licence, and the following season Vitória increased his
responsibilities, putting him in charge of their Under-18s
as well as the Under-16s. His work impressed the coach,
Manuel Fernandes, who was to influence his career
greatly. Manuel Fernandes had been an international
centre-forward of distinction, with twelve years at
Sporting Lisbon before ending his playing career at
Vitória and being invited to stay in Setúbal and succeed
the veteran English coach Malcolm Allison. In 1990, after
two years in charge, Manuel Fernandes joined Estrela da
Amadora, a club on the outskirts of Lisbon who had just
seized their first major trophy in more than half a

century's existence by winning the Portuguese Cup final – and took Mourinho with him.

Mourinho's job as assistant with the title of fitness coach meant he would be working with senior players for the first time. But it was an ill-starred venture. Estrela were relegated at the end of the season and both Manuel Fernandes and Mourinho lost their jobs. At least Mourinho had gained a modicum of European experience at the age of twenty-seven – Estrela overcame the Swiss club Neuchâtel Xamax on penalties before succumbing to FC Liège of Belgium in the second round of the Cup Winners' Cup – but whether that was any consolation as he returned to Setúbal can only be a matter of conjecture. Things were to look up, however, and when once again he took the helping hand of Manuel Fernandes fate had something much, much better in store. Manuel Fernandes had been in Ovar, a small town in the north that was later to acquire a measure of sporting distinction through the success of its basketball team, and worked for the local club, Ovarense, and it was during this apparently low point of his professional life that he received a call that was to transform a career. Not his – though he was soon to be back in the top division – so much as Mourinho's.

Mourinho, then, was to be liberally rewarded for the wisdom he had shown in getting those qualifications in Scotland; they were necessary if he was to have any realistic hope of progressing to the heights he envisaged.

But why did he have to go abroad for them? Surprising though it may be, given his own country's contribution to the game, Portugal did not subscribe to the mainstream European coaching curriculum, as used by around forty member countries of UEFA. And why specifically Scotland? 'Coaches came here from all over the world,' recalled Tosh McKinlay, a former Celtic and Scotland player destined to encounter Mourinho later. 'When I was sixteen or seventeen, they used to ask me to go down – they needed young players as sort-of guinea pigs for their training exercises – and I can remember seeing the great Italian coaches like Fabio Capello and Arrigo Sacchi as well as our own, led by Alex Ferguson.' So José Mourinho, having taken advice as to where he should seek his certificate, applied and was accepted for the annual summer course of the Scottish Football Association, held at Largs on the Ayrshire coast.

He arrived with two other Portuguese students and was assigned to a group of fellow foreigners, Americans and Europeans in the main. There were more than 150 students in all, and one of the assessors that year, the former Scotland forward Paul Sturrock (now Sheffield Wednesday manager), said: 'He didn't stand out. In fact, I can't remember him.' Sturrock's erstwhile international colleague Gordon Strachan was also there, starting out on the new career that was to take him to Coventry and Southampton before he moved to Scotland to succeed Martin O'Neill at Celtic. Strachan, too, scratched his head. 'You are put in groups of twelve on these courses,' he said, 'and don't really mix with people from other groups unless you stroll down to the pub for a chat in the evening. Maybe José didn't go to the pub.' Andy Roxburgh remembers the student Mourinho. Just. Roxburgh was Scotland's national coach at the time and he told me: 'I've spoken to José about it since and what he remembers is being impressed that the national team manager of Scotland was also taking the coaching courses.' Yes, but what did Roxburgh himself remember? 'It's very difficult for me to recall every detail of everyone who was on a course.' His assistant Ross Mathie, who remains an SFA stalwart to this day (Roxburgh has for several years been technical director of UEFA), was the course director that year. What's more, he was looking after the international group of aspirants. He said: 'I can definitely picture these three Portuguese guys. In fact, I recall José having a photograph taken with Andy. But I'd be leading you up the garden path if I pretended there was much more I could add.' So, in summary, it is fair to say that Mourinho's impact on his teachers and fellow students did not lead them to conclude they had been favoured by the presence of greatness.

He had, however, obtained the first half of the requisite certificate at the age of twenty-five and felt the better for it. 'I went back to my young players at Setúbal,' he was later to tell Roxburgh, 'and, because of what I had learned, made a difference.'

Twelve years after that first visit to Largs, he returned – in the extraordinary interim, Mourinho had worked with Bobby Robson and then Louis van Gaal and sat alongside them on the bench while Porto and Barcelona collected trophies galore – to complete his qualification for the UEFA licence. Normally a coach does the two parts of the course in consecutive summers, but Mourinho had been too busy learning at football's university of life, acquiring experience more valuable than any piece of paper as his status (and salary) soared and he worked daily with the likes of Luís Figo, Rivaldo and Ronaldo. He did, however, want that certificate. And, being out of work, he was free to go and get it. So he flew back to Scotland. He could afford business class now.

Among the other students in the European Championship summer of 2000 were Gary Bollan, then a Scottish Premier League player with St Johnstone, who would become a player–coach at a lower level with Clyde; and Tosh McKinlay, who was playing for Kilmarnock at the time and has since filled a variety of roles from agent to radio analyst. They remember Mourinho. 'As soon as he walked on to that training pitch,' said McKinlay, 'you knew he was different from the rest of us. It was how organised he was, and the way he put things across.'

The students gathered on 24 June, as the European Championship in Holland and Belgium reached the quarter-final stage, and that evening Mourinho watched on television as Portugal beat Turkey 2–0. All four quarter-finals – the other matches ended Italy 2 Romania 0, France 2 Spain 1 and Holland 6 Yugoslavia 1 – were used by Ross Mathie for match-analysis tests. The students sat in the lecture theatre at the Inverclyde Sports Centre with pens and notebooks at the ready and, watching a large screen, logged the matches. Mourinho was on his usual form. He sailed through the exam. As you would expect. 'I was in José's group,' said Gary Bollan, 'and it was immediately obvious that he had come with a coaching background. When he did training exercises, he was much more firm and outspoken than the others. He exuded confidence in his own ability. There was no hesitation, no self-doubt. Of course we'd heard he'd been at Barcelona with Bobby Robson and all that. But José never brought it up, never bragged about it even when we popped down to the pub after finishing for the day. He was a good lad. Very down-to-earth.'

McKinlay agreed: 'It was inspiring to hear him talk about football. We had quite a few chats. One night during the course, they have a dinner and I was sitting next to him. I started by asking him about Jorge Cadete, the Portuguese striker I'd played with at Celtic – José knew him from Sporting Lisbon – and we got on to all sorts of football stuff. Three years later, I bumped into him at Ibrox.' By then Mourinho was in charge of Porto. 'He'd come to Glasgow to watch Celtic play Rangers shortly before they met his team in the EUFA Cup final. I wasn't sure if he'd remember me because he'd become so successful since we last met, but he comes over and says, "Hi – how are you? What are you doing here?" I explained that I was doing a bit of work for Celtic TV. I wished him good luck for the final but added, "You know where my allegiances lie!" He just laughed. Since then I've seen him on the television a lot and I just love listening to the guy because he talks sense.'

Having charmed the Scottish FA's class of 2000, Mourinho flew home with his certificate. At last he was a qualified professional coach. And in the next few years he was to go it alone in spectacular style, winning the national championships of both Portugal (twice) and England, plus each of the two European titles. Plus four domestic cups. Succeeding, indeed, with such an intensity as to make even a Robson or a Van Gaal gasp.

No wonder much is still said of the benefits of a Scottish education.

Mourinho had, of course, availed himself of quite a bit of supplementary tuition between 1988 and 2000, thanks to his relationship with Manuel Fernandes. Sporting had recalled their erstwhile star forward from Ovar as assistant coach in preparation for the arrival of a big-name foreigner. The trouble was that the new boss, an Englishman, spoke no Portuguese. Manuel Fernandes was talking it over with the president who had invited him back to the club, José Sousa Cintra, when a solution occurred to him: why not engage José Mourinho, who spoke very good English and could act as interpreter?

Sousa Cintra readily agreed and, Mourinho having been sent for, the trio went to Lisbon airport to meet the flight from London. Eventually a familiar face came through customs. Mourinho stepped forward. 'Hello, Mister,' he said. For the first time. The first of countless times. Because that is what you call a head coach, regardless of his nationality, in Portugal, and Spain and Italy for that matter. The British taught the world to play football. So, just as the British use the French word for a cook, some nationalities defer to the original masters of the game of football. Sir Bobby Robson, a most patriotic Englishman, never minded that.

'Hello, Mister.
I'm José Mourinho'

Actually what Mourinho said to Bobby Robson upon greeting him that day at Lisbon airport was: 'Hello, Mister. I'm José Mourinho.' And, after handshakes, he went on to explain why he would not be hurrying off. Robson had had little idea of what he would encounter in a country he had hitherto known only as a very pleasant holiday destination. Of course he knew a fair amount about Portuguese football: he had played against Portugal twice in England's successful qualifying campaign for the 1962 World Cup, and, when England manager, had endured the disappointment of a 1–0 defeat by the Portuguese during the opening phase of the 1986 tournament in Mexico. But he did not know the language. So he was glad to hear this smart young man speak English with such clarity and confidence. Meanwhile an older man, short and tanned and neatly dressed, stood to one side, smiling broadly. 'I am speaking,'

Mourinho continued, 'on behalf of the president.' He gestured to the older man, who extended his own hand, and Robson was introduced to Sousa Cintra, his new employer.

On the drive into the city, Robson reflected that it could have been a worse start. 'Two things struck me straight away,' he said. 'The standard of José's English. And the fact that he was a nice-looking boy. Too good-looking for my liking! I remember telling him one day when we were having photographs, "Don't stand next to me, José – you'll make me look ugly."'

Mourinho was supposed to be an interpreter plain and simple. Sousa Cintra's plan was for Manuel Fernandes to be Robson's right-hand man. As soon as Robson had signed his contract in England, the president had announced to the Portuguese media that Manuel Fernandes would return to Sporting as the Englishman's assistant, presumably in order to reassure fans that the club's traditions would be observed. 'Manuel Fernandes could not have done the number-one job,' said Robson. 'He wasn't quite a good enough coach at that level. His previous job had been with Ovarense, who have never been in the first division. They are what we'd call a Conference-sized club, I suppose. But he was a very popular figure both within the club and among the fans. José had been working as a schoolteacher and doing a bit of coaching with him. So they'd come to Sporting to be my back-up.'

It was almost inevitable that the language issue would make Robson lean towards Mourinho. 'He was there with me on the pitch every day. Behind me. While I picked up a little bit of Portuguese.' Hitherto Robson had worked only with English or English-speaking players in his homeland, and Eindhoven, where he went after parting company with the national squad following the World Cup semi-final defeat by Germany on penalties in 1990, was hardly a problem because English is widely spoken in Holland. 'Working with the Portuguese players on the pitch wasn't really a problem for me either – once I'm out there, I've always been able to get by – but every now and again something has to be explained carefully. José was very good. He listened, learned, looked, remembered. He was bright, alert and intelligent. But what I liked best was that, when I'd indicate a player and say to José, "Tell him this, tell him that," I always had the feeling that José was saying it the way I would have said it. That was his knack. He knew he had my backing so he'd tell a player to get closer to his opponent or push up a bit more and they'd respond as if I'd told them. I could see – it was the same reaction. Whether it helped that he came from a footballing background, I don't know, but he had a true bond with me. Also I said to him, "José, I want to know every word these players are saying in the dressing room, what they're saying about the team, and the tactics, and about me. Whatever Figo is muttering about me, you bloody well tell me." '

Those players included Jorge Cadete – later to share the Celtic dressing room with Tosh McKinlay – as well as Luís Figo, who, though young, was already demonstrating the rich talent that was to make him Portugal's most capped footballer of all time. So Mourinho became Robson's eyes and ears. And mouth, on occasion. 'If I was upset with any player, or needed to get a point over strongly, José wouldn't pull any of my punches. There's always a temptation for an interpreter to do that, but José was very assertive. He never watered down the message. He wasn't afraid. Even with Figo.'

The words Robson used to describe his aide's playing prowess – when, being a man short for an eight-against-eight or nine-against-nine in training, he would tell Mourinho to get a bib and take a certain position – were 'keen' and 'enthusiastic'. It was meant kindly. 'He had a certain amount of fitness and, through working with the players, developed it. So, when I used him as a fill-in player, he did all right. When we later went to Barcelona, in fact, he'd be on the same pitch as not only Figo but Ronaldo, Hristo Stoichkov, Pep Guardiola and all the other fantastic players.' Could he move among such company without risking embarrassment? 'Mmm. For a short period. For a twenty-minute practice period. He couldn't do it in a match! But no, he didn't embarrass himself.'

Sporting did. They sacked Robson before his first season was out. Sousa Cintra took a snap decision when

Carlos Queiróz (later to become Sir Alex Ferguson's assistant at Manchester United) became available. Manuel Fernandes was shown the door too, as was Mourinho, the pair walking together once more. But Sporting had made a mistake that was to play straight into the hands of their rivals Porto. Shortly afterwards, while Robson was still in Lisbon, he met Mourinho for lunch and declared that Porto had made him an offer. 'José just gasped. "Mister," he said. "Don't let that pass you by. You must go there." And he told me why, explained what a great place it was for football. I asked him if he'd like to come and he said he'd love to.'

At Porto, Robson truly established himself as one of English coaching's most successful exports, emulating his Dutch achievement by winning the national championship twice in a row. And again Mourinho was by his side. On an enhanced salary of £35,000 a year, which was to keep multiplying until, at Barcelona, he became football's highest-paid interpreter. 'I never gave him a coaching job,' said Robson. 'He *assisted*. He expressed my instructions to the players. I never handed the team over to him, even for half an hour, in all the years he was with me. But during our time at Porto he began to offer suggestions. I'd arrive in the morning and say, "José, we're doing this and this, you've seen me work, you know how I want it done," and he might chip in with an idea or two. He was growing into the job.'

Mourinho, in his application to take the Scottish FA

course in 2000, stated that he had been 'assistant coach' with Robson at Porto and that was not taking too much of a liberty. 'I did what an assistant coach is meant to do,' he later told an interviewer, 'and with Robson, who lives and breathes for the pitch, that meant planning training sessions.' In fact he did more than that. Robson had noticed that he was a good reader of the game and decided to send him to spy on forthcoming opponents. 'He'd come back and hand me a dossier that was absolutely first class. I mean first class. As good as anything I've ever received. Here he was, in his early thirties, never been a player, never been a coach to speak of either, giving me reports as good as anything I ever got from the top professional people I'd brought in to scout for me at World Cups when I was with England – Dave Sexton, Howard Wilkinson, the lot. There would be the way the teams played in the match he'd been sent to – both teams – with defence and attack covered very well, patterns of play, nicely set out with diagrams and a different colour for each team. All as clear as a bell. I remember telling him, "Well done, son."

'I think he enjoyed being with me. He loved being on the training pitch and, because I'd come to respect him as a student of the game, I'd sit him down after matches and we'd have long conversations. We'd talk about who'd played well and who hadn't, where we'd gone wrong and what we could do about it.' Several years later, their paths having diverged at Barcelona, Robson was to be in his native north-east of England, reviving Newcastle United, and Mourinho back at Porto, doing much the same thing, this time as the boss, surrounded by his own coterie of assistants. During his first spell at the club, the president, Jorge Nuno Pinto da Costa, had noted his capabilities both on and off the training pitch, said Robson. 'In all my dealings with the president, I'd taken José in with me and he'd fought on my behalf. The president obviously took a shine to him during those meetings. Also he remembered what happened on the pitch in our time. Two championships and a Portuguese Cup in two seasons – you can't do much better than that. And José was by my side all the way. No wonder the president kept an eye on him.'

Porto initially continued to thrive after Robson's departure in 1996 for Barcelona (though a lean spell was to follow, opening the door for Mourinho to return to the club). Robson had had no hesitation in inviting Mourinho to join him in the new adventure at Barcelona, one of the greatest clubs in the world, let alone Spain. Indeed the only condition Robson laid down before taking the job was that Mourinho came too. Once again he was to be multi-functional: every time Robson met the Barcelona president, Josep Lluís Núñez, or vice-president, Joan Gaspart, he would be there. The master and his voice were now friends and, when Robson set up home in Sitges, just down the Mediterranean coast from Catalunya's capital, Mourinho did likewise; he could afford it, too, on a salary that would rise to more than £300,000 a year.

'We saw each other socially,' said Robson. 'My wife, Elsie, became friendly with his wife, Matilde, and we'd all go out for meals together in the evenings. The talk always turned to football. Quite soon after we sat down, usually. What did the wives think? Oh, they understood. They'd just give us a look that said, "Uh-oh, here we go again." Matilde had some interest in the game, a slight knowledge, and sometimes they would listen to us, but she and Elsie were never too intrusive. Basically, they would talk about their things and we would talk about football.'

In the mornings, Robson and Mourinho would drive into the city, to a training ground lying in the shadow of the Camp Nou, a massive stadium holding more than 100,000 spectators, to exercise Barcelona's thoroughbred players. At first it was a trial for Mourinho, who, unlike Robson, had no standing in the game. 'They didn't know who he was – and made that quite plain. Also they questioned whether, not having been a player of any standard himself, he was entitled to be telling them what to do. But he won them over.' Gradually, the key figures in the dressing room came to accept he had a lot to offer: skilfully edited videos, for instance, illustrating strengths or weaknesses of opponents, were especially appreciated by the more thoughtful players. Josep Guardiola, an elegant ringmaster on the field, was one who valued

Mourinho's work. Guardiola, known as 'Pep', was a Catalan, which served to embed him in the supporters' hearts. 'He was a big fish,' said Robson. 'A good player too. He had his opinions on the game, Guardiola, and I didn't mind that. He'd say we couldn't play this way or we couldn't do that – he had an opinion on everything. José saw that he was an important figure within the club and said to himself, "I've got to get to know him, I've got to get in with this guy." And he did. José and Pep were quite friendly. They respected each other. And, of course, José could speak to Pep.' In Spanish or, eventually, Catalan.

'José gradually built up a rapport with the squad. The players liked him. He even joined in a bit of banter with them. He got close to Ronaldo, which helped.' The young Brazilian was to become the biggest name in the game – world and European player of the year – after Barcelona took Robson's insistent advice to buy him from PSV Eindhoven, a former club of Robson's. 'Ronaldo took to José quite quickly. José was in a good position with the players generally because he didn't pick the side – I did. So, if a player was left out, he blamed me, not José. I had to keep a distance from the players, as a manager does. José could cross over that line and come back again.' He did too. As at Sporting Lisbon and Porto, he would spy on not only the opposition's players but, at Robson's behest, his own team's. Take the case of Hristo Stoichkov. 'A strange one,' said Robson. 'I'd been worried about Stoichkov.' The greatest Bulgarian footballer ever,

Stoichkov had a reputation for living up to his dark and brooding appearance. 'I'd heard he was a difficult character to have around the club. Yet I found him quite the opposite. He was a pro who didn't muck about in training – he trained right and played right. I'd thought he'd be a surly, unsmiling, unsociable Iron Curtain type. He wasn't. And José got very friendly with him. So did I in the end. But José knew him better because José would mix with the players. He and Stoichkov were very friendly. They used to talk about the team a lot. And José would pass it on to me. But I liked Stoichkov and I trusted him.'

Just as Mourinho had overshadowed Manuel Fernandes at Sporting Lisbon, he was closer to Robson than the ostensible number-two at Barcelona, José Ramón Alexanco, a former club captain. In Robson's one season in charge of the team, 1996–97, Barcelona won the European Cup Winners' Cup, beating Paris St Germain in the final through a Ronaldo penalty, and the Spanish Cup, but finished two points behind their arch-rivals Real Madrid in the championship. Robson nevertheless assumed this would be enough to persuade Núñez and the other directors to let him fulfil the second year of his contract. He was wrong. While the financial terms of the contract would be honoured, he was to give way to Louis van Gaal, the Dutch coach who had guided Ajax to the European title two years earlier. He was to become 'general manager' and take other duties, such as travelling the world in search of suitable talent. Suddenly Barcelona had in Mourinho and Robson not only the most lavishly remunerated of interpreters but, as Robson himself ruefully put it, 'the world's highest-paid scout'.

He went to a meeting – accompanied by Mourinho, naturally – with Núñez, Gaspart and Van Gaal and expressed his disappointment. But Van Gaal was assured by Robson that, if the president saw him as Barcelona's future, there would be no further dispute between them, and Van Gaal said he appreciated that. Robson, already in his mid-sixties, was to have further coaching posts at PSV, again, and Newcastle. What, though, was to become of Mourinho? His first instinct, said Robson, was to quit, head home to Portugal – 'José didn't like what had happened to me' – and ponder his future. But Robson went to Van Gaal and advised the Dutchman to keep Mourinho. 'I told him, "Louis, he knows the city, he knows the club, he knows the players. He speaks fantastic Spanish and can do for you what he's done for me. He's an asset." So he stayed with Louis. And he got to do a little more work. A bit of coaching. That's because Louis is different from me. I have to be in full control, hands-on. Louis is one of those guys – the Sven-Göran Eriksson type – who like to stand back. Louis would even hand over the team to José for friendlies. That was great experience for him.'

In the summer of 1998, Robson went to Eindhoven, where there was no job for Mourinho (it was a short-term assignment). Robson rang to tell him so and advised Mourinho to keep learning under Van Gaal. Until the following September, when Newcastle sacked Ruud Gullit and brought Robson out of retirement. Again he rang Mourinho. 'I said, "There could be a job for you here at Newcastle, but I'll have to get my feet under the table first. In the meantime, work out what you want to do." ' By the time Robson was ready to make him an offer, almost exactly a year later, Mourinho was on home soil, waiting for a suitable club and ready to be judged as a coach in his own right. 'He asked me what I thought. "Give it a go," I said.' He did. He got the Benfica job. And lasted just three turbulent months. 'When I heard he'd gone from Benfica,' said Robson, 'I thought maybe the job had been too much for him, that he wasn't quite there yet. But there were reasons for his leaving which explained it.' Club politics, essentially.

I asked Robson what he had had in mind for Mourinho at Newcastle and he replied: 'I just saw him as an important member of the staff. I saw him scouting, doing match appraisals, looking at players. But I also envisaged using him on the training pitch every day, giving him more responsibility on the coaching side and letting that develop.' No doubt many Newcastle supporters have fantasised about what might have happened to their club had Robson groomed Mourinho as his successor, prepared him to command a stripe-shirted institution as passionately supported as Porto but with more of the resources required to finance a Champions League campaign. According to Mourinho, that is what Robson laid on the table, without even tempting him to take it seriously; he simply could not believe that Robson would ever stand back from the team until he retired from football completely, and told him so. Robson recalled a less clear-cut proposal: 'Obviously it was understood that he'd be maturing all the time and I'd not be getting any younger. But I'm not sure that I saw that level of capability in him at that stage. I mean it. It wasn't a question of doubting him. I knew he was bright. I knew he could handle players. I didn't know he had enough technical knowledge to be his own man.' Surely the thought had occurred, however fleetingly, when Mourinho handed in those spot-on scouting reports, that here was a tip for the top? 'One thing doesn't necessarily follow the other. And, as far as being a principal coach is concerned, I didn't know he had any ambition in that direction.' Amazing. Such reticence from the young man we were to see, just a few short years later, relentlessly destroying all the giants of the profession could strew in his path – and boasting about it. 'He had humility then,' said Robson. 'Throughout the time we were together, he showed me respect. He knew what my position was and where he stood. He never tried to rise above his station.'

There was a story that, when they were at Barcelona, players who understood English formed an impression that Mourinho was not simply translating Robson's

Rebel with a cause: according to Desmond Morris, the ideal actor to play Mourinho would be James Dean (*Coloursport*).

All together now: a feature of the Mourinho regime is the *bonhomie* between players and staff, here exuded by Damien Duff, Frank Lampard and Mourinho (*Getty Images*).

Mourinho's father, Felix (*above left*), was the first to recognise and nurture his talent as a coach. Later José continued his education with Sir Bobby Robson, who took him to Barcelona to work with great players such as Ronaldo – here helping Robson to show off the European Cup Winners' Cup – and Louis Van Gaal. The Dutchman broadened Mourinho's experience by allowing him to take charge of the team from time to time (*Empics & Coloursport*).

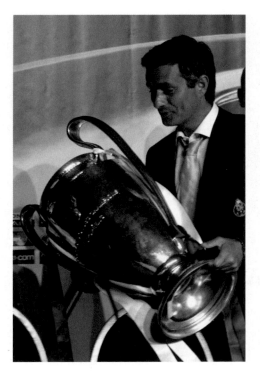

The special ones: Mourinho with the Champions League trophy after Porto's triumph over Monaco in May 2004 and, just five weeks later, at Chelsea with his closest aides (from left): fitness coach Rui Faria, scout André Villas Boas, goalkeeper coach Silvino Louro and assistants Stevie Clarke and Baltemar Brito (*Empics & AFP/Getty Images*).

A man for all seasons: Mourinho and Newcastle assistant Dean
Saunders watch through the sleet as Chelsea go out of the FA Cup
at St James' Park. In the warmer conditions offered by Tel Aviv,
Mourinho addresses Israeli and Palestinian coaches. At Liverpool,
after the final whistle has sounded on Chelsea's Champions League
campaign, there are congratulations for the victors (*Empics*).

Barcelona moments. Drained but happy: Mourinho with Joe Cole after the aggregate victory (*Empics*). Trouble brews as Anders Frisk, the referee in the Nou Camp, falls out with Didier Drogba, whose red card Mourinho mentioned in the comments that indirectly led to Frisk's retirement (*Coloursport*). And at Bolton in the spring there is joy as Frank Lampard's second goal seals the title (*Empics*).

One of the boys: After Chelsea have clinched the Premiership title at Bolton, John Terry gives Mourinho the sort of hug a player gives to another. In the background are Frank Lampard and Didier Drogba (*Empics*).

Happy family: Mourinho with his wife and children at the UK
première of the film *The Incredibles* in London in November 2004.
The Mourinhos have followed an old Portuguese custom by passing
on their Christian names to their offspring; the son is called José
Mario and the daughter Matilde. In order to avoid confusion, they
have nicknames (*Getty Images*).

instructions but amplifying them slightly. Did he ever suspect that? Robson grinned. 'Well, I wouldn't know, would I? No, I never had the feeling that the message was anything other than precisely as I'd intended. José did a great job and he was very loyal to me.' Nor did Robson notice the cockiness, the contentiousness towards opponents or the propensity for getting up people's noses. Not much anyway; there was a tunnel fracas after a match against Athletic Bilbao when the Basque club's coach, Luis Fernández, was said to have pointed a disapproving finger at him. But the Mourinho who was to be presented to the sports fans of Portugal and with whom we, the English audience, were to grow familiar – the unpredictable, sometimes exasperating and almost always enthralling Mourinho – had yet to rise to the surface of his personality. As Robson said: he had humility then.

A little bit of arrogance

Louis van Gaal did not blame Mourinho for getting upset with Barcelona over their treatment of Bobby Robson. He was speaking to me in Sitges, in the apartment he retains there; he and Mourinho were neighbours. 'It was a strange situation when I arrived,' said Van Gaal. 'I had initially been engaged as director of youth development. Then suddenly the president changed his mind and wanted me to be coach with Robson in charge of scouting. Now Robson had won three trophies in the season just finished. But, being a gentleman, he didn't show his anger. Mourinho showed anger! His position would be disappearing as well, of course, because as coach I would be bringing my assistants from Holland with me. But when we had this meeting with Núñez and Gaspart I was encountering Mourinho for the first time – and I was impressed with his personality. I knew I needed help with Spanish, having had only one week at a language school in the Netherlands, so I told the president it would be convenient if Mourinho, who also knew the players, would stay as my assistant, my third assistant [behind Gerard van der Lem and Frans Hoek, who had worked with Van Gaal at Ajax]. So he was kept on, initially for a year. To start with he was just a translator, but gradually he became as valued as my other assistants. He could read the game and he analysed the opposition so well that, after my first year, when we won the Spanish championship and Cup, I was happy for him to stay for three years.'

In the second of those years, he worked with the first team. 'I like to give responsibility to my assistants,' said Van Gaal. 'I like them to take all or part of a training session because, if the head coach trains the players all the time, in the end they stop listening to you. A coach has to observe and correct, but there is only so much correcting you can do before, psychologically, they switch off. So sometimes I like to stand back. But in order to do that you have to be confident in the quality of your assistants. In José's case, I started with him by my side. Then, as is normal, we divided the players into three groups – Frans Hoek with the goalkeepers and the others split between Gerard van der Lem and José – and once I had seen how José handled it I knew I could trust him. I am a believer in ball possession and positional play. So we do a lot of positional play in a session. Then you can see if someone can really coach. And he could. He could see what the players had to do. Also there was the quality of his analyses. The players saw them and, if players get the feeling that the coach can read the game better than they themselves can, they listen. I decided he was good enough to take charge of the team in friendly matches. He did a lot of those, plus games in the Catalan Cup, which could be not so friendly because Barcelona's local rivals, Espanyol, and the lower-division clubs took them seriously, as did the media.' Van Gaal was always present, lest any of his players be tempted to doubt Mourinho's authority. 'This was my only reservation,' said Van Gaal. 'I'd see enough to know he could really coach. I'd seen him give the talks to the players at half-time. If I had felt the need to intervene, I would have done. I just didn't know if he could do it when I wasn't there. To get to the very top, you must be able not only to organise players but handle a team, to find that chemistry. That's the difference.'

Van Gaal, like Robson, never noticed in Mourinho a burning ambition. 'I never even noticed a restlessness. But then we were a team. We spoke about what he did – not what he wanted. Maybe he spoke about it to other people.' Although Van Gaal has a reputation for being stern and dour, he and his wife, Truus, enjoy their time off and they would get together with the Mourinhos for meals or children's birthday parties. 'I know the journalists think I don't like to socialise,' said Van Gaal, 'but I do. José and Matilde, who became close friends with Truus, had an apartment in the same park as ours, so, if he was late in completing his analysis of our next opponents, he'd just bring it round and stay for a chat. I liked him. He was a little bit arrogant, not always a respecter of reputations, but I like that. I like people with a high opinion of themselves and like to surround myself with them. I don't want yes-men, because you need people who will say, "No – there is another way." He could do that. And he did. I encouraged it. I told him to include in his analyses how *he* would play against this opposition. I have always stimulated that sort of contribution but, because of José's special qualities as an analyst, I paid a little more attention to him than my other assistants in this respect. And, OK, it's always the head coach who decides how the team will play – but I certainly wanted to hear José's point of view.'

The truth, by Mourinho's own account, is that he had become restless at Barcelona, impatient for the power to direct operations, beset by a curiosity to discover if he could follow in Van Gaal's footsteps and be his own man. Van Gaal regards the football the team played in his third year with Mourinho as the best of his time in charge, even though they failed to complete a hat-trick of Spanish championships and lost to Valencia in the semi-finals of the Champions League. 'It was just that we had a lot of trouble with Rivaldo, who had been voted world player of the year and decided in the middle of the season that he didn't want to play on the left side any more. Because he refused to play where he was asked to play – because, in effect, he withdrew his labour – I left him out of the team, and the disruption it caused meant we didn't quite fulfil our potential. There was a lot of criticism of the president and he quit. Out of loyalty, I quit also. The assistants had to go too. Especially Mourinho.' When I expressed surprise, Van Gaal chuckled. 'I sometimes think I was the only guy who believed in José. Because, when Robson left and I insisted José had to stay, they weren't pleased. He was known as *El Traductor* [The Translator]. The media called him that. When I first came to the club, even the president called him that, but I always spoke about José as a football man and gradually all the officials started to treat him with the respect due to one of my assistants. I took him more seriously than most people in the club, I think – because I was in a position to judge him.'

Benfica's loss is Porto's gain

When Mourinho returned to Portugal in June 2000, it was to a state of unemployment. Very much self-imposed, to judge from his version, which was that he had no wish to stay at Barcelona, being unimpressed by their choice of Llorenç Serra Ferrer as Van Gaal's successor. He did not believe the Majorcan, who had been working with the club's youths, had much chance of success at the higher level (Ferrer was to be dismissed after eleven months) and was reluctant to work under him. Van Gaal doubted that the new man would have wanted Mourinho around anyway: 'I'd installed Serra Ferrer as head of youth education and I don't recall he and Mourinho had a good relationship.' What's more, Mourinho had grown tired of the subordinate's life. In the last of his three years at Barcelona, he had become increasingly frustrated and had often come home to his wife in grumpy mood as he analysed Van Gaal's decisions and compared them unfavourably with those he would have taken. His mind was made up: he had to be number one, even if it meant taking a big drop in pay.

He had a reputation in Portugal. While in Barcelona, he had received the odd offer from his homeland, the most attractive from Sporting Braga the previous year, and he imagined some such middle-range club would suit him best. Mourinho was in no hurry – he had built up a respectable bank account while in Barcelona – and spent the rest of the summer either at his home in Setúbal or in the Algarve, where he had bought a holiday place near Portimão. There were football books and videos to study and there was time to start collating his thoughts on coaching in a computer document for strictly private use, which, presumably without a hint of irony or embarrassment, admirers have come to call his 'bible'. There was a family to enjoy – his daughter was four and his son a baby – and the sun shone.

September came and Mourinho, having spurned Robson's offer to come to Newcastle, was in Setúbal when the phone rang. On the line was Eládio Paramés, a former football journalist who had become director of communications at Benfica. He told Mourinho the club's president, João Vale e Azevedo, had a proposition to put. Mourinho, aware Benfica already had a coach, Jupp Heynckes, said he was no longer interested in being anyone's assistant, but Paramés persuaded him to see the president, who confirmed that the job on offer was the German incumbent's.

Although you could hardly call Benfica a humble beginning for Mourinho's career as a coach, the club had fallen a long way from the heights occupied in the years of his infancy: the Eusébio years, when they could look any European club in the eye. They were skint and struggling and could barely keep pace with the likes of Sporting Braga, let alone their great rivals Sporting and Porto. But there was still the Benfica name, with all it entailed in terms of tradition and size of support; Mourinho had to give the president a hearing. Vale e Azevedo told him the club indeed had no money, so he wanted Mourinho to build a team with hungry, young, Portuguese – or, to put it another way, cheap – players. Oh, and the contract would be for only six months because there was an election for the club presidency coming up (the leaders of most clubs in Portugal, and Spain for that matter, are chosen by the members) and that would take place in a matter of six weeks or so. That was the bad news. The good news was that Vale e Azevedo was expected to win and, as and when that happened, Mourinho would be given a two-year extension. Mourinho took the chance, took the job. Vale e Azevedo lost the election.

The winner, Manuel Vilarinho, had run on a ticket that proclaimed Benfica's next coach would be Toni, a former star player, and Vilarinho's first statement was that he hoped Mourinho, being a man of honour, would recognise his duty to step aside, so it could be said that their relationship was getting off to a tricky start. But Mourinho, after receiving an assurance from Vilarinho that he could continue until at least the end of the season, got on with the job. He made the players train less casually and railed at the backroom staff for providing dodgy dossiers – one report listed only ten men in the opposition's team – and generally strove to change the club's culture. Then, in his ninth match, they achieved a remarkable 3–0 home victory over Sporting. Few victories are sweeter than in a derby, yet the taste can turn bitter when a coach is consumed by righteous indignation and, as Vilarinho appeared at the door of Mourinho's office while he was speaking on the phone to his wife, the president was ignored. Furthermore, Mourinho declined to speak to the press, assured Benfica staff he would pay the ensuing fine and drove home.

Next he attempted to force Vilarinho's hand. He asked for a year's extension to his contract, on the pretext that another club had expressed interest in him – and the reply could be most charitably described as lukewarm. Yes, said Vilarinho, I'd happily keep you on; it's just that some of the other directors, and our commercial partners, are not sure. It was agreed that Mourinho would leave immediately. His team's derby triumph had a more orthodox consequence when Sporting's coach, Augusto Inácio, was sacked. And guess who moved into that job? Manuel

Fernandes, Mourinho's old friend and partner, the man who had recommended he be hired as Bobby Robson's interpreter. Toni, of course, got the Benfica job. So Mourinho's first solo flight was all too quickly over. It had lasted barely a couple of months. But, as Robson later said, the circumstances had made that almost inevitable.

It was nearly Christmas. Almost exactly four years before Mourinho and his wife were to take the children ice-skating near Sloane Square in London.

Mourinho waited at home in Setúbal until mid-April, when he took a call from a representative of the União club of Leiria in the Portuguese midlands and agreed to take over from Manuel José at the end of the season. Leiria were already doing well and finished fifth that season, their highest position ever, but Mourinho had them in fourth place as, once again, Christmas approached and things started happening. Benfica sacked Toni and offered Mourinho his job back – he declined after it became clear there was no room at the club for Baltemar Brito and Rui Faria, who had become the first members of a team of assistants destined to share in his fame – and then Porto beckoned. The president, Jorge Nuno Pinto da Costa, had assured him at an international match in Oporto several months earlier that he would take command when the time was right. Just after Christmas, an intermediary's call informed him the time had almost arrived and in January he replaced Octávio Machado.

Porto, like Benfica, had a proud history. They, too, had been champions of Europe. Just once, but more recently than Benfica – in 1987. The current Porto team, said Mourinho, was their worst for twenty-six years – he would have remembered the mid-1970s, for in those days Porto frequently trailed in behind Vitória Setúbal, whose Bonfim Stadium was his second home and for whom his father kept goal – but no matter, Mourinho added: 'Next year we'll win the League.' They did.

For the first time since he had attained headline-commanding status, Mourinho had done what it said on the tin. He had begun to rebuild in the remaining months of his first season, setting up deals to bring in the likes of Maniche, Nuno Valente, Paulo Ferreira, all of whom went on to represent Portugal, and Derlei, whom Mourinho had found in Brazil while preparing for his time at Leiria and brought to that club at a knockdown price. Cast aside, sometimes quite unceremoniously, were those he perceived to be of faint heart or unsuitable head. The broad strategy was to make the team more Portuguese in character and hungrier (through incentive-based contracts) and early in the new season he made a tactical switch to the 4–4–2 formation with which European glory was to be seized. He had fashioned a disciplined, resilient unit. But Mourinho's Porto were already more than that. In Deco, also born in Brazil but to be claimed by Portugal, for whom he was to take part in the 2004 European Championship, they had an artful playmaker and he was prominent as Porto proved they also had the sophistication to operate successfully outside Portugal's borders by winning the EUFA Cup after a long and, on occasion, turbulent campaign, the bargain buy Derlei finally putting paid to Celtic with his eleventh goal in the competition. While Porto's players celebrated in front of their fans, very much a minority in Seville's Olympic Stadium, some 40,000 supporters of the Scottish champions indicated by scornful gesture that Mourinho's men were a bunch of divers (in truth, though Deco and company were not unacquainted with the art of obtaining free-kicks, the frequency with which they fell had as much to do with Celtic's rough approach). Mourinho had supervised a remarkable, and merited, triumph.

He did get one thing wrong. Asked how his team would cope with the even greater rigours of the Champions League the following season, he replied: 'We can do some nice things . . . but I don't think we can win it.' He explained that such aspirations were only for the 'sharks', whom he defined as 'clubs who can afford to spend 20, 30 or even 40 million euros on one player'. Porto hardly caused a ripple in the market that summer. Yet, with virtually the same team, they went on to win the Champions League. So had Mourinho's modest assessment been a psychological ploy, designed to take the pressure of expectation off his players? Not this time. I think that, for once, he genuinely surprised himself and only developed a conviction they could defeat the odds after the dramatic survival of a second-round visit to Manchester United, where, a linesman's decision having crucially gone their way, Costinha scored a stoppage-time winner and Mourinho wildly celebrated on the touchline.

A less judicious man might have missed it all by leaving after the UEFA Cup triumph. He did briefly consider the possibility of cashing in. Inevitably, there were offers from abroad that would have doubled or tripled his salary: from Paris St Germain and a couple of mid-range Italian clubs. Among those confidants he consulted was Robson. 'I told him to stay another year,' said the Englishman, whose Newcastle had just finished third in the Premiership, a position that meant they could themselves qualify for the Champions League if they beat Partizan Belgrade over two legs, which they were clear favourites to do. 'I told José, "You've got time on your side. Don't get into a cage unless you know how to get out of it. You're not ready to move yet. I was at Ipswich fourteen years – you've been at Porto barely fourteen months! So stay for at least a year. Apart from anything else, the president has taken a chance with you. Yes, you've done well for him. You've had a wonderful year. But you might learn more next year if you stay and get more experience." ' It proved good advice. Meanwhile Robson was unable to join Mourinho in the Champions League. Newcastle, after winning 1–0 in Belgrade, succumbed by an identical score at home and lost the penalty decider. Oddly enough, the subsequent draw for the group stages put Partizan in with Porto; fate was that close to laying on a contest between the erstwhile master and his pupil (it was never to happen, for after Mourinho came to the Premiership his first encounter with Newcastle took place three months after Robson had been sacked).

As it was, Porto had to deal with Real Madrid as well as Partizan and Olympique Marseille. If the big and financially muscular clubs of Europe could be likened by Mourinho to sharks, Real were the Great Whites of the European game; they did not even recognise his 40–million-euro limit, having spent nearly twice as much on the world's most expensive player, Zinedine Zidane. Other *galácticos* who came to test Porto included Roberto Carlos, Mourinho's old Barcelona chum Ronaldo and an even more familiar face: Luís Figo. They won 3–1. It looked as if Mourinho's analysis of the relationship between money and Champions League success was right; Porto had been severely bitten. But they healed their wounds by beating Marseille twice (the French club were later to remove poor Robson's Newcastle from the UEFA Cup) and qualified for the knockout stages in second place.

Although they came from behind to beat Manchester United with two goals from Benni McCarthy in the new Dragão Stadium, they were not expected to preserve the lead in the face of a shark attack at Old Trafford and duly Paul Scholes put United in front midway through the first half. Later Scholes scored again, or would have done had the linesman not erred in ruling him offside. 'Porto would never have come back from 2–0,' said Robson, 'and that was the only major slice of luck they got in the competition.' Given that United led on the away-goals rule, it would still not have been enough but for Costinha's swift reaction to a rebound off the United goalkeeper, Tim Howard, as the majority of a 67,000 crowd prepared to celebrate the final whistle. As Mourinho put it: 'My team were out after ninety minutes – and in the quarter-finals after ninety-one.'

Lyon were next and the decisive manner in which the French were overcome sharpened appetites for the semi-final against Deportivo La Coruña. The first leg, at Porto, was dull and goalless, but Mourinho and his team did not appear too despondent and a fortnight later, on a stormy night by the Bay of Biscay, we discovered why: they clearly believed they could win at the Riazor, even though Milan, the reigning champions, had been thrashed there in the previous round. With Costinha shackling the creative abilities of Deportivo's elegant Juan Carlos Valerón, the opportunity was there for an away goal to settle matters. Deco – slippery as an eel, persistent as a terrier – did the trick after an hour, tempting the stand-in defender César to try a tackle the Spaniard was not sharp enough to execute legitimately and falling just inside the penalty area. Derlei did the rest. Porto were in the final. It was to be against little Monaco, who had not only removed Real Madrid but were to deny a Chelsea backed by the billions of Roman Abramovich. So much for Europe's sharks. It was the year of the minnows. Well, the smaller fish. You know what I mean. Mourinho, like the rest of us, had underestimated the power of football to overcome economics. It must have been the only thing he had neglected to learn during his prolonged and comprehensive education.

By now he was Chelsea's choice for the next season and this, despite the Italian alternative presented by Internazionale of Milan, was an offer he could hardly refuse. Peter Kenyon, having been unable to get Sven-Göran Eriksson to Chelsea, was falling on his feet. After the match in La Coruña, Mourinho, brow furrowing as he fiddled with his mobile phone – 'at moments like these, you want to speak to your loved ones' – declined to discuss his future, but the next morning he flew from Oporto to London with his wife and children and in the evening, accompanied by a posse of Portuguese journalists, he went to Stamford Bridge, where Monaco's second-leg victory in the other semi-final ensured that the Champions League would not be culminating in a contest between his present and future employers; it must have been quite a relief, even to such an expert exuder of indifference as Mourinho.

Next there was some domestic business to attend to. The retention of the Portuguese championship had already been achieved but the task of keeping the Cup in

Porto loomed, with a final against Benfica due ten days before the European climax in Gelsenkirchen. Mourinho, aware that Monaco's coach, Didier Deschamps, would be watching, altered and slightly weakened his team, who were reduced to ten men in the second half when Jorge Costa was sent off. They nevertheless played well enough to be level at a goal each after ninety minutes, but Simão Sabrosa scored for Benfica in extra-time and afterwards Mourinho decried the referee's performance. He was quoted as having called the official – Lucílio Batista, from Mourinho's own home city of Setúbal – a cheat, but Batista's report referred only to constant querying of decisions from the Porto bench. It was not a first offence. Mourinho was ordered to pay a fine of 600 euros, which the records of the Portuguese Football Federation show him to have duly done, and to serve a suspension of fifteen days, which he avoided by leaving Portugal for England. Via Germany.

The event in Gelsenkirchen was affected, as Mourinho generously volunteered afterwards, by an early injury that deprived Monaco of their captain, Ludovic Giuly. 'It changed the face of the match,' Mourinho said, 'and enabled us to play the football we like to play.' Which was on the counter-attack. Carlos Alberto got the first of three unanswered goals in the first half and, after Dmitri Alenitchev had replaced the Brazilian youngster on the hour, Deco, with a piece of deliciously impudent finishing, and the substitute put Monaco out of their discomfort. The scenes at the end were of the usual delirium, except that Mourinho had a subdued look and stayed close to his wife and children. He also chose not to exhibit his medal, removing the ribbon from his neck after the presentation, and later told Andy Roxburgh: 'On a personal level, the night was difficult because I was full of conflicting emotions, knowing that I would be leaving the team – I did not see my Porto players again until three months later when they came to Stamford Bridge in the Champions League.' Apart from Paulo Ferreira and Ricardo Carvalho, that was; he wasted no time in bringing them to Chelsea and tried to lure Deco, who chose Barcelona instead. Mourinho had become a shark.

Before embarking on his predatory activities, he revisited London to brief Chelsea staff and agents and meet the media, who, upon asking why he was so confident about the prospects for a club who had last won their domestic championship eight years before he was born, responded: 'We have top players and – excuse me if I'm arrogant – a top manager . . . please don't call me arrogant, because it's not true. I think I'm a special one. I'm a champion.' Having also dealt with more esoteric matters, such as the balance of responsibilities within his coaching department (we did not trouble our newspapers' readers with that), and outlined his disciplinary code (we printed it, albeit without reference to its uncanny similarity to that of other coaches), he flew to Brazil for a ten-day family holiday. The midsummer he spent commenting for a Portuguese newspaper on the European Championship, which was being held in his homeland. How strange to reflect that he had watched some of the previous European Championship in Scotland while completing his coaching qualifications; now he was the most fêted coach in the world! Then he took his new charges off to the United States to prepare for a season that, being Mourinho-influenced, was bound to be momentous.

Until that late-May evening on which Mourinho's previous season reached its glorious conclusion, the abiding image had been of his touchline dance in his overcoat at Old Trafford. In my mind this was superseded by the tutorial Mourinho gave Alenitchev in the technical area shortly before he ran on to the field to take over from Carlos Alberto. It lasted several minutes and involved much pointing at a notepad. Usually a substitute gets little more than a quick word and a pat on the bottom; Mourinho's attention to detail was fascinating. Fifteen minutes and two goals later, the job was done. The following spring, while Mourinho was carrying all in England and Europe before him, a seasoned observer of the game told me he was overrated. 'What he does,' my friend opined, 'is painting by numbers.' Such respect does my friend command that I lacked the heart to reply that, if that were the case, we should all be doing it, and picking up several million pounds a year for our trouble.

PART THREE

José who?

The three hats

Andy Roxburgh, whose job it is to monitor the work of the coaching profession's most distinguished exponents, says José Mourinho is the product of an advantageous upbringing and an ideal education, supplemented by 'the finest example of work experience in the history of employment'.

Apart from that, he never had much going for him.

When Roxburgh visited him at Chelsea last year, Mourinho made a wry quip: 'After fifteen years, I'm an overnight success.' The UEFA technical director understood. It is less important for a coach setting out on his career to be instantly recognisable to millions than to have learned the elements of his craft. The fame and fortune that go with being a star footballer can mask an inability to cope with the retraining process. Mourinho was once asked why so many players who had failed to reach a high level, either through injury or for other reasons, went on to succeed as coaches. His reply was swift and simple: 'More time to study.' While the game's chosen ones are still playing, the rejects are learning and, increasingly, they are landing the top jobs.

In this respect, then, Mourinho is nothing special. Among those who have coached teams to Champions League or UEFA Cup honours after playing careers ranging from the unsung to the barely existent are Arrigo Sacchi, Ottmar Hitzfeld, Rafael Benítez and Gérard Houllier. Marcello Lippi, Louis van Gaal and Sir Alex Ferguson, though respected professionals in Italy, Holland and Scotland respectively, were never called to represent their countries. Brazil's triumph in the last World Cup was overseen by a non-international: Luiz Felipe Scolari. So was Greece's in the European Championship: by Otto Rehhagel. It is the same farther afield. The moves in the South American championship final were plotted by Carlos Alberto Parreira of Brazil (who won on penalties) and Argentina's José Pekerman, both what you might call career coaches. Indeed, of the ten leading football nations in the world, only two had former international players in charge of their squads at the end of last season. Germany had placed their trust in Jürgen Klinsmann and Holland in Marco van Basten. By and large, those who employ coaches are coming to understand that it is a specialist job for which the ability to send a crowd into paroxysms of delight with a swivel of your hips is not necessarily the prime qualification.

When Roxburgh became Scotland's coach, he was greeted by 'Andy Who?' headlines. Which, given that his entire playing career had taken place in Scotland, right under the headline-writers' noses, must have been slightly hurtful. But he was in good company. The English newspapers had much the same reaction to Arsène Wenger's appointment at Arsenal. 'There is still a public perception,' said Roxburgh, 'that in order to be a competent coach you have to have been a famous player. But it's not always the case. There are many examples of very famous players – wonderful, instinctive players – who were absolutely useless as coaches or managers. Then you have the reverse – people like Arrigo Sacchi. He wasn't even a professional player.' Yet he built, at Milan, one of the best club sides in the history of the European game. And then guided Italy to the World Cup final in 1994. When they lost on penalties to a team supervised by Carlos Alberto Parreira, who had never kicked a ball professionally either. 'Now I'm not denying that to have been a top player is an advantage,' Roxburgh continued, 'if the other attributes are in place.' As in the cases of, say, Johan Cruyff, or Fabio Capello, a distinguished attacker with Juventus and Italy who, having succeeded Sacchi at Milan, immediately established himself as an outstanding coach. 'The top player starts with the experience and the players immediately respect him and listen to him. But it is only a start. Guys like José and, before him, Arrigo Sacchi have had to earn that respect. They've had to work even harder than the former star player.'

Houllier loves to quote Sacchi on this topic. Asked how he could coach without having played, the Italian replied: 'I didn't realise you had to have been a horse to be a jockey.' The functions were completely different, said Houllier: 'When you are a player, you focus on your career. When you are a coach, you focus on everything. Stuart Pearce was eloquent about it. He said that, when he became a player–manager at Nottingham Forest, it hit him like a revelation.' It did not put him off permanently, for Pearce, having obtained his qualifications and worked under Kevin Keegan at Manchester City, has taken responsibility for that club's fortunes. Maybe he will make the transition. Houllier's playing habitat was the French third division and subconsciously, he said, he might have been driven to compensate for unfulfilled dreams by developing the instinct to organise others. Like Mourinho, he was lucky to have paternal guidance. 'My father was in charge of a local team near Boulogne and showed me how to do things. When I was a player, I started going to analyse the opposition, just for fun mainly, though the coach did find it helpful. José has spoken highly of his father and what he gained through being the son of a coach.'

Even as he approached the end of his time at university, Mourinho would do the occasional spying stint for his father. Félix, his coaching career having peaked in two spells at Rio Ave – the latter featured an appearance in the Portuguese Cup final, which Porto won 4–1 – began moving from one lower-division club to another, usually involuntarily. Still José stayed close to him. But the young Mourinho had to think about earning a living and even then he took a direction that served his future interests well, as Roxburgh explained: 'He had trained to be a teacher.' Again Roxburgh, as a former teacher, might be biased, but he insisted there were countless examples of how a teaching background could help to prepare a coach: to name only a couple of the more prominent Dutch ones, Van Gaal and the late, revered Rinus Michels. 'Rinus would always say his teaching background had been invaluable. After all, teaching is about communication and organisation – and so is coaching. Then, having established that building block in his career, José went to find the next, educating himself in coaching by going on courses like the one he did with us in Scotland. This gave him the global method of training, which he still uses.' It involves the development of technical, tactical and fitness elements together, through the medium of compressed small-sided games, and, said Roxburgh, had been formulated by the SFA to suit the mentality of Scots, who 'get easily bored and don't like drills and things like that'.

More than a decade later, when Mourinho took charge at Leiria, he surveyed the location for pre-season training with the president, who gazed at the nearby hills and valleys and observed that they would be ideal for running. Mourinho told him to forget the scenery; the players would be running only on the pitch. Did that resonate with Roxburgh? 'Absolutely. Our mentality was all to do with the pitch. It was portable goals and small-sided games, double-penalty-box games, wingers' games – an endless stream of games. The players would be learning without realising it. José has, of course, had many influences along the way. But he still has this global view. At Chelsea his fitness trainer, Rui Faria, will rarely work detached from the coaching itself. He will stand beside José and advise him on decisions about when to extend the pitch or widen it, or highlight a certain aspect, or increase the intensity of an exercise, change the speed, make it two-touch or whatever. Everything is done together.'

Robson introduced him to a different approach. 'With Bobby,' said Roxburgh, 'he could begin to learn like a fly on the wall. Bobby used to give the first period of training to an English fitness coach called Roger Spry, a great guy who had worked in Brazil and was wonderful on movement and so on. Then Bobby would do the tactical stuff. It was perfect for José just to be there and take it all in. In our course for the UEFA pro licence, the most important thing is the practical work. The students must attach themselves to a club for a week and shadow the head coach. Then our tutors go and watch them and help them. José was learning that way week after week, month after month, year after year. I went over once to make a film for UEFA and could see that he was totally integrated in what Bobby was doing. He would have learned a lot about man-management, because Bobby's brilliant at that. Then, at Barcelona, Louis van Gaal moves in. Totally different. While Bobby's what you might call a romantic of the game, Louis is highly structured, very much of the Dutch school. And José gets this whole new education in how to structure a day's training. Even better, he gets practical experience through being handed the team for matches. At half-time Louis would go into the dressing room with José, not to talk to the players but to listen to what José was telling them. Then later he'd discuss it with him. So now he'd gone way beyond the shadowing phase. He was actually managing a team – Barcelona, remember! It was like the ultimate finishing school.'

So he went back to Portugal and put it all into effect. Mourinho himself has traced his rise to international prominence back to Porto's UEFA Cup quarter-final against Panathinaikos in 2003. Having been beaten 1–0 in the home leg, his team had to go to a stadium where the Athens club had never lost in European competition. But one goal from Derlei took the match into extra-time and another from the Brazilian striker won it. 'That changed the mentality of the club,' said Roxburgh. 'José felt he'd arrived and he was proved right as Porto went on to beat Celtic in the final.' After that, Roxburgh had organised a forum of his elite coaches and decided to break with tradition by inviting the finalists from the UEFA Cup as well as the Champions League. 'Both José and Martin O'Neill came and José's first contribution was amazing. Here he was, the new kid on the block, round the table in our boardroom in Switzerland with the Capellos and Lippis and Fergies and Wengers and all the other stars. One of the first questions was "What do you think of the silver goal?" ' This was the rule whereby, if a knockout match were drawn after ninety minutes and a team led at the end of the first fifteen-minute period of extra-time, the second period would be abandoned and the match end then. It has since been scrapped and the two periods of fifteen minutes restored. But Porto had won the UEFA Cup on a silver goal, scored by Derlei in the 115th minute of a final during which Henrik Larsson had twice equalised. 'There was quite a lot of debate and people like Marcello Lippi said they preferred two times fifteen minutes. José listened to it all. And then he made his contribution. "I thought it was a very, very interesting thing," he said, "to train my players to cope with that." He had nothing to say about whether it was a good or a bad rule. To him it was just another challenge. He was asked what he meant. He replied that he had told the players to imagine two different fifteen-minute scenarios. In one they were winning, the other losing. How would they handle it? Because those few minutes might be all they had to win the match. That told me everything about José as a coach. He wasn't voicing negative opinions about the rule – it was there, and he would train his players to make the most of it.' Similarly, he has been known to make his players practise *attacking* with ten against eleven – just in case they ever have a man sent off in a match they need to win.

A proverb adapted from Thomas Carlyle states that genius is an infinite capacity for taking pains and, while it might not be universally applicable in football, Mourinho's career does evoke it. On the one hand, there is the occasional detractor like my friend who considers him a painter by numbers. On the other, there is a regiment of admirers such as José Manuel Capristano who, when vice-president of Benfica, initially regarded Mourinho as too inexperienced to handle the first team but was won over in a matter of weeks and exclaimed: 'That man was born to be a coach. I have never met anyone like him in my life. He thinks twenty-four hours a day.' Or Deco, who has said: 'Maybe other coaches have the same quality as Mourinho – but nobody works as hard as him.' Roxburgh recognised that reluctance to leave a stone unturned. 'I must have said it a thousand times. The guys I deal with, either the national coaches or the top club guys, are *obsessed* with detail. That's what makes them different. Louis van Gaal, for example. I remember him coming to one of our meetings – he was at Barcelona with José at the time – and complaining that, in the Champions League, the gap in time between the warm-up and the kick-off was too long. He told me to get it changed. Now, it was only a minute too long, two minutes at the most. But he was insistent. So we changed the countdown. These are tiny details. But they matter to such people. José's very much like that.'

Preparation is fundamental to Mourinho's approach. And writing things down. Anyone watching Sir Alex Ferguson would sense that here was a man who liked to live on the edge, to improvise, to rescue situations with a bold substitution (or two, as in Barcelona in 1999, when Teddy Sheringham and Ole Gunnar Solskjaer turned an impending Champions League final defeat by Bayern Munich into glorious victory). Mourinho leaves the absolute minimum to chance. 'He does have that instinct for the game,' said Roxburgh, 'but he prefers to do as much as possible through preparation. He is also very good – and this would have been honed with Van Gaal – at analysing his own team's games. José says this. You watch him in the first half of a game. He's got a little pad and he takes notes. Only in the first half. He doesn't do it in the second half. Some people like to take notes, others to use little tape recorders. Fergie, incidentally, does neither. He's got perfect recall, a photographic brain – that's why he's so good at quizzes – but José likes to jot down what he calls his little reminders. By the time he goes in to see his players at half-time, he's talked to his assistants and got his talk ready so the points he wants to make can be punched out. The reason he doesn't take notes in the second half is that he's not going to speak to them at the end. He doesn't think that works. He prefers to go off and analyse it later.'

Today, with the aid of technology, coaches exchange information more than ever before. So I asked Roxburgh if, at his forums, he had noticed a certain convergence. Were the top ones becoming much of a muchness, all preaching the same dogma? Or did Mourinho's achievements mark him out as a man apart? 'It's a hard question to answer,' he said, 'but I don't think they are all alike.' There would always be differences of emphasis. 'I remember being involved in the tsunami-relief match in Barcelona and our dressing room contained an array of talent beyond belief. Everywhere you looked there was a great player. You'd think that, when you get to that level, one would be as good as the other. But they've all got their own personalities and specialities. David Beckham is different from Ronaldinho. And they perform at their peak when the environment is right. If you look at coaches, Marcello Lippi's record proves he is high class – "Lippi's got us all beat," Fergie keeps saying – but when he went to Inter it didn't work. Different qualities suit different contexts. It's a matter of chemistry. José Mourinho might not be the right guy for Juventus. Yet they've all got the same tools today. They've all got these computer systems and analysts and expert advisers all around them. They've got psychologists – well, some do and some don't – and the ability to monitor their players' fitness. These things are only back-up. It's how they use the tools, how they relate the information to football players – and that's such a delicate, fragile relationship.' So what puts the best above the rest? 'They wear three hats.'

Three hats?

'Selector. Coach. Manager.'

In the past, Roxburgh explained, before the supervision of professional teams became as developed and scientific as it is today, many of the top people were good at selection and management but modest in their knowledge of training methods. 'Now look at Alex Ferguson or Arsène Wenger or José Mourinho. They wear all three hats and they wear them well. They can *select*, which means more than just picking and balancing your team. It means deciding which players to buy in order to improve your team. It means choosing your scouts – so your club can choose which players to buy and discover new talent – and the other backroom staff. Then there's the *coaching* hat, which entails training people to be better and gelling them into a team. To get the *management* hat, you have to be able to handle the players, to maintain discipline and order and so on. Certain people stand out at certain things. Fabio Capello, for instance, is brilliant on discipline. But he definitely has three hats. And there's no doubt in my mind that José has all three.' One difference between them, of course, being that, while Capello began with a name, Mourinho had to make his. But Roxburgh insists that renders Capello an exception to the rule. 'I actually think the majority of the top coaches are guys who have had to think, and work at it. Guys who have a sympathy for the learner. The ability to deliver a pass and the ability to deliver a message – these are completely different things.'

Selection

José Mourinho always had an eye for a player and a system. Otherwise his scouting reports would not have found such favour with Sir Bobby Robson, let alone satisfied Louis van Gaal, whom even his best friends would consider as fiercely demanding a coach as any on earth. And Mourinho, upon being given the opportunity, wasted little time in using his judgement. While waiting to take over at Leiria, he travelled to Brazil and came back with a couple of players, Derlei and Maciel, paying far less than they proved to be worth. At Porto, he rebuilt quickly, cheaply and to dramatic effect. But Chelsea was a different sort of challenge: the budget was huge and expectations in proportion. And what he was being asked to fix was not exactly broken because Claudio Ranieri had steered the team to second place in the Premiership and the Champions League semi-finals. Mourinho went about it in his usual businesslike way, sending Roman Abramovich, Eugene Tenenbaum (the owner's right-hand man) and Peter Kenyon a computer presentation with lists of players he wanted to retain, discard or recruit and the infrastructure he required. (Being aware that Chelsea's scruffy training ground near Heathrow Airport had come to serve as little more than a joke among the players, he was reassured to learn that a sparkling new facility was under construction at Cobham in Surrey and would be in use within weeks.) All was agreed on Abramovich's yacht.

Already there were reports that Mourinho would be going back to Porto for three of his European champions and, at his inaugural press briefing in London, I asked if they were true. He shook his head and said there might be one signing from Porto. 'I don't need players I know,' he stressed. Englishmen such as John Terry and Frank Lampard would be relied upon as before. 'I don't need to bring in players for protection. When I was at Barcelona with Louis van Gaal, he kept bringing in Dutch players. This is something I don't want. It shows two things. That you are not so self-confident as you think – it's like a young boy who goes on holiday with his parents all the time because he is afraid to go on his own. Also that you are not such a good professional if you only know players from your own country.' It was a stirringly forthright answer: one of many that were to keep us agog through the coming months. Perhaps it would have been less well received, however, if we had realised it was utter piffle. Four of the first seven players Mourinho signed were from Portugal and it would have been five out of eight had he landed Deco, who chose to go to Barcelona instead. Even without Deco, he took two from Porto – Paulo Ferreira and Ricardo Carvalho – as well as Tiago from Benfica and the youngster Nuno Morais from Penafiel. All were represented by his own agent and confidant, Jorge Mendes, so the transfers were hardly bolts from the blue. On this occasion, Mourinho must have been reading from the wrong tin. Or maybe, as a relative newcomer to the world of wheeling and dealing, he made his error through an inadequate grasp of the art of obfuscation. He still has some difficulty, thank goodness, with that.

'When you take over a club,' said Gérard Houllier, who supervised the modernisation of Liverpool before making way for Rafael Benítez, 'you have to build and maintain three teams – the team that is playing, the team that is *not* playing and the team behind the team.'

The first team had already begun to take shape in Mourinho's mind. Carlo Cudicini was in place and Petr Čech was arriving from Rennes to challenge him. Paulo Ferreira and Ricardo Carvalho would join John Terry in a defence stiffened by the presence, just in front of the centre-backs, of Claude Makelele. The other midfield positions would be contested by Tiago, Joe Cole, Geremi and Alexei Smertin with Damien Duff and the most exciting of the new boys Kenyon had secured in advance, Arjen Robben, supplying width. Eidur Gudjohnsen would play a little off the front. Behind Hernan Crespo. The Argentine, though, was to be the subject of a joint reappraisal. When the players reported for duty at the old Imperial College training ground, Crespo was a notable and unexplained exception. When they were handed Mourinho's guide to behaviour and ethos, the copy intended for Crespo went unclaimed. 'From here, each practice, each game, each minute of your social life must centre on the aim of being champions,' it read, ending with a line that might have come from Lord Kitchener: 'I need all of you.' Two days later, Crespo strolled in from South America, mumbling excuses about flights. He was called into Mourinho's office, given a vibrant lecture and asked if he would settle in England and give the same commitment as the rest of the players. He declined and was loaned to Milan, though Crespo was to return in time for the 2005–06 season. And Chelsea promptly smashed their transfer record in paying Olympique Marseille £24 million for his replacement, Didier Drogba.

The non-playing team, the group of players on the fringes who would have to be kept motivated through spells of inactivity, Mourinho addressed with a clear-out. The last thing a coach needs is malcontents. But sometimes the cost of getting rid of such players when they are in mid-contract can be daunting. Mourinho was lucky. His club could afford to pay them off. Crespo was a good example in the sense that, with wages in Italy under sharp downward pressure, Milan were unwilling to contemplate paying his salary of £4.8 million for the year. So Chelsea gave them two-thirds of it. (Had Chelsea reached the Champions League final, they would have been paying him twice as much as Milan – to play against them.) They had already shipped Juan Sebastián Verón to Inter in a similar loan deal. Off to Birmingham on permanent transfers went Mario Melchiot and Jesper Grønkjaer. Middlesbrough took Jimmy Floyd Hassel-baink. With retirements and less significant departures, the squad was cut to a manageable size: twenty-three senior players. Given that two or three of these would be injured most of the time, the potential for grumbling would be minimal. And Mourinho would be working only with players who had a reasonable chance of contributing to matches, even in a small way; there would be no clutter, no wastage of effort, and that is exactly the environment in which Mourinho likes to coach.

As for the team behind the team – as Houllier referred to the back-up staff – Mourinho had already assembled most of them. He began to form his inner circle of assistants while preparing to go to Leiria. Although only too eager to test his 'methodology' after a somewhat false start to his solo career at Benfica, he sensed a requirement for an enforcer, someone who could deal with the players. His wife suggested Baltemar Brito and Mourinho has worked with him ever since. Brito is more than an assistant; he is one of Mourinho's closest friends. They have known each other since the Brazilian, a tall and bow-legged central defender, gritty and reliable but of limited technique, played for Mourinho's father at Rio Ave in 1981–82; José, remember, was a junior member of that squad. Brito is joint 'assistant manager' at Chelsea. But some assistant managers are more equal than others and Brito, rather than Stevie Clarke, seemed to take charge when Mourinho was unavoidably absent from the bench during Chelsea's Champions League run. Clarke, though, has clearly been accepted into Mourinho's group. The former Chelsea defender, a Scot, is one of few surviving connections with the past and his initial function was to point Mourinho to areas which had been neglected under the Ranieri regime, such as youth development. He is the ideal link man.

Then there is Rui Faria, the fitness coach whom Mourinho inadvertently exposed to ridicule during the Bayern Munich matches by appearing to use him to pass messages and, in Germany, face the press; one columnist referred to him as 'puerile', another called him a 'woolly-hatted halfwit'. After Brito, he is the next longest-serving member of Mourinho's circle. When Mourinho was assisting Louis van Gaal at Barcelona, a student from the sports university in Porto got in touch, seeking help in completing his final papers. How could Mourinho, himself a graduate of the corresponding establishment in

Lisbon, refuse? They got on so well, furthermore, that when Mourinho joined Leiria, the former student, Rui Faria, was beckoned.

Silvino Louro, like Brito in his mid-forties, looks after the Chelsea goalkeepers, as he did those of Porto; Mourinho found him there when he arrived from Leiria. Setúbal-born, Silvinho had the most distinguished playing career of the group. He played twenty-three times for Portugal in goal and twice appeared for Benfica in European Champions' Cup finals: in 1988, when PSV Eindhoven beat them on penalties and Hans van Breukelen, his opposite number, was the hero; and in 1990, when, coached by Sven-Göran Eriksson, they lost to a Milan goal scored by Frank Rijkaard.

André Villas Boas has the title 'assistant coach/scout' and an air of mystery that transcends it. At Porto he was called something like 'director of opposition intelligence'. Villas Boas is Mourinho's spy. He watches and analyses opponents, just as Mourinho used to do, and prepares dossiers to be handed to the players, normally twenty-four hours before matches. He too deals in detail, supplying rundowns on each possible opponent, including what kind of runs the player likes to make, whether he favours the left or right side, whether he likes to dribble or pass, his stamina levels, capabilities in the air and temperament. Another thing Villas Boas has in common with the young Mourinho is that he aspires to be a head coach; not long after coming to London, he happened to mention it. Mourinho was not pleased and told Villas Boas to stop speaking to the press. Perhaps it is just as well. Publicity and intelligence work can be strange bedfellows.

A quick glance at an internet site containing a brief biography of Villas Boas, however, leads us to believe he has a British grandmother – not unusual in Oporto, due to the port trade – and coached youths at Porto before turning up as technical director of the British Virgin Islands FA in 1999 . . . when he was twenty-one! Sir Bobby Robson remembers him at Porto. He was in his teens when Robson was coach there and used to wait outside the Englishman's apartment. At first the boy wanted just an autograph or a chat and Robson obliged. But, when he asked for a job on the Porto staff, the response could only be a gentle refusal. Villas Boas wrote to Robson at Barcelona, repeating his request for a start in the game. He must also have kept in touch with Mourinho, for, when Mourinho took charge at Porto, he turned up on the staff, ready to follow in his footsteps. He, too, must be a good analyst. Just as Robson and Van Gaal trusted Mourinho, Mourinho trusts Villas Boas. Maybe the British Virgin Islands job came too soon for him. He is remembered there also. The president of the British Virgin Islands FA between 1996 and 2000, Kenrick Grant, told me: 'His plans were very impressive on paper and so we gave him a job as youth director and assistant to our head coach on 350 US dollars a week plus expenses. But he was always very quiet. He'd had the privilege to be around the top people in Portugal, apparently, and never really settled or got focused here. Whenever he had the opportunity, he'd go back to Portugal. One time, he wrote to me asking for a reference and I said I was sorry but I could not do that. He never came back to us. I was really surprised to hear he was with a top team like Chelsea.'

Not for nothing has Villas Boas been called 'Mini-Mourinho'. He took a prominent role in his master's feud with Frank Rijkaard. Amid the euphoric scenes as Stamford Bridge prepared for Pierluigi Collina to blow the final whistle on Chelsea's victory over Barcelona, Villas Boas swaggered towards the visitors' dugout and said something that irked Rijkaard, whom a steward restrained. As the Barcelona players trooped off, Villas Boas was still apparently taunting them and Samuel Eto'o motioned to him to shut up. As again a steward intervened, bundling Eto'o away, Villas Boas stood triumphant, sneering. It was not an edifying sight.

All of these people, from the unassuming Brito to young Villas Boas, must be treated respectfully by the Chelsea players. Mourinho, who was afforded the same courtesy by Van Gaal at Barcelona, insists on it. The first commandment of Mourinho's 'bible', the document hidden in his laptop which sets out his coaching principles, apparently insists that no individual must be greater than the club (a tenet which any benevolent dictator would find convenient) and the team behind the team have their own status. Each member is there because Mourinho feels he can trust him. Trust is fundamental to what he calls his 'methodology'. But upon arriving at Chelsea he needed to be able to trust his lieutenant on the field more than anyone and so his choice of captain was a key decision.

Under Ranieri the role had been taken by Marcel Desailly, with John Terry deputising when the great but somewhat creaky French defender was taking one of his frequent rests (Desailly retired just before Mourinho's arrival). When Chelsea flew to the United States for their pre-season tour, Terry was only twenty-three but an established member of the England squad who had taken the suspended Rio Ferdinand's place alongside Sol Campbell in Sven-Göran Eriksson's defence during the European Championship and done well. Mourinho sat beside him on the plane crossing the Atlantic and confirmed he would keep the armband. 'He told me what he wanted from me as captain,' said Terry. 'He told me that, on the training pitch and around the place, he wanted me to be a speaker and out there in games he wanted me to get his words across to the players.' The consequences of that decision were long to echo around a united, vibrant dressing room; Mourinho had picked just the man and, towards the end of the season, players up and down the country recognised it by choosing Terry as the Professional Footballers' Association Player of the Year.

So, having selected a lean squad with a strong leader, Mourinho needed to choose the right tactical framework for them. At Porto he had favoured a tight midfield diamond: in other words, 4–4–2 without wingers. At least that was what he had shown us in the Champions League, when Porto were often facing teams such as Real Madrid or Manchester United who had more players of outstanding individual accomplishment; he would some-times use a different formation against inferior sides in Portugal. The requirement to switch for the Champions League he explained thus: 'To win we had to go about things in a certain way. If you have a Ferrari and I have a small car, to beat you in a race I have to break your wheel or put sugar in your tank.'

At Chelsea, initially, he appeared still to be suffering from small-car syndrome. 'They started with a diamond and people were saying they were a bit dour,' recalled David Moyes, whose Everton lost each of their matches to Chelsea 1–0. After nine Premiership fixtures, Mourin-ho's team had scored a mere eight goals. But they were without Arjen Robben and his arrival on the scene, belated due to the first of his injuries, changed every-thing. In their next nine matches, they scored twenty-nine goals and developed a new system. 'I don't know if he stumbled on it or what,' said Moyes, 'but good managers do that. They find a system that suits their players and, when Robben came into a side that already had Damien Duff, they had two top-class wide players. So Mourinho developed this version of 4–3–3.'

Whatever circumstances called for, he would supply, notably in the Champions League: against Barcelona, lightning-quick counter-attacking; against Bayern, long high balls towards Didier Drogba, an old-fashioned English centre-forward who happened to come from the Ivory Coast. In the Premiership, one memorable act of boldness occurred in the west London derby with Fulham, who were drawing at Stamford Bridge when Mourinho threw on Robben and moved Duff to left-back, which meant Chelsea had no fewer than six attackers on the field. There were, moreover, forty-five minutes to go. But fewer than ten of those minutes had passed when Duff surged forward and prompted Robben, whose perfectly laid ball Frank Lampard stroked into the net. Mourinho then adjusted the balance of the team again, replacing Drogba with the midfielder Tiago, and Chelsea won 3–1. In Ranieri's day this had been called tinkering; now it was tactical acumen. Only against Liverpool at what proved the end of Mourinho's Champions League campaign did he fail to come up with a solution to Chelsea's difficulties, which were probably due to mental bluntness as much as anything else, the second leg having fallen three days after the Premiership had been clinched at Bolton. What he could choose he chose wisely. But he could not always pick his moments.

Coaching

David Moyes suddenly grinned. 'What Mourinho's done,' said the Everton manager, 'is make coaching sexy.' He was alluding less to his rival's good looks than to a tendency to use fancy words and phrases to describe his methods. One of these is 'guided discovery', by which Mourinho means that players at a certain level must be led gently to lessons rather than told what to do; it is an approach he learned at Barcelona, one he shares with, among others, Sven-Göran Eriksson. On the other hand, we hear from John Terry, he is not above barking to his Chelsea charges: 'Hey – don't fuck about!'

In an interview with Andy Roxburgh for UEFA's coaching magazine soon after he joined Chelsea, Mourinho described his coaching style as flexible and evolutionary – 'I am different today from five years ago' – but very demanding in terms of the commitment required from the players during training. 'I have always been lucky to have more than one pitch at my training centre,' he said, 'and I therefore prepare my sessions in such a way that I can jump from one situation to another with effective working time high and resting time very low. We go for quality and high intensity during short periods. Players want to work, whether it is in Portugal, England or Spain, as long as the training is well organised and serious and they know the purpose of the exercise.

'When I went to Scotland in the late 1980s, after finishing my studies, your methods made me think about methodology in a different way. The way you used small-sided games to develop technical, tactical and fitness training – a global view of training. I believe in the global method. My fitness coach works with me on the tactical systems, advising on time, distance and space. I want to develop tactical aspects of the game: how to press, when to press, transitions, ball possession, positional play. After that other things come – the physical and psychological aspects are part of the exercise. The individual work is done when we feel the players need that. Often we need to separate the players into groups depending on their condition and the amount of playing time they have had. The emphasis of the work is always tactical.'

It's not always so sexy, then, but the players do swear that they love their briskly conducted work with Mourinho and, by his side, Rui Faria. And, while there is no shortage of public testimony – 'training is enjoyable every day,' says John Terry, 'and you learn so much' –

the best evidence is what they say privately. As the anecdotal evidence built up over Mourinho's first season, the former Arsenal striker Ian Wright said he had been told even the players on the fringe of the first team enjoyed training – 'and that is a major achievement'. Meanwhile Gérard Houllier, whose post-Liverpool role as expert analyst of English football on French television kept him in touch with the Premiership grapevine, told me: 'Believe me – the players just love Mourinho's coaching and man-management.' The two linked together, of course, in accordance with the global principle.

In Tel Aviv, Mourinho told his audience: 'A great pianist doesn't run around the piano or do push-ups with the tips of his fingers. To be great, he plays the piano. He plays all his life and being a great footballer is not about running, push-ups or physical work generally. The best way to be a great player is to play football.' That said, he added, a good coach must know more than football. 'He has to be a leader of men and a coherent leader. He must make all his men feel big, not small.' A compact squad is helpful in this context.

The influence of Louis van Gaal at Barcelona is clear from Mourinho's tactical syllabus – possession and positional play have always been central pillars of the Van Gaal method – but the Dutchman has noted a divergence on philosophy. 'He has more belief in defence than attack,' said Van Gaal. 'My philosophy is always –

because I believe we must entertain the public – to have attacking play. *His philosophy is to win!* That is the difference.' This is not to brand Mourinho a philistine. He has gone out of his way to deny that, for all his belief in match analysis and preparatory work, he sees football as a science rather than an art; like most coaches, he considers the game a combination of the two. But he has no time for unnecessary embellishment, and a much-lauded example of his individual coaching has been his trimming of those fussy frills from the game of Joe Cole, who has emerged from the process as a regular and productive member of the England team.

In Mourinho's first few months at Chelsea, he was often exasperated by Cole and his tricks. An erstwhile boy wonder at West Ham, the twenty-three-year-old Londoner seemed perpetually to be trying to vindicate his early publicity, which had hailed him as a new George Best, an English answer to Diego Maradona, and all the rest of the usual suspect theories. What Cole usually turned out to be was a very gifted midfield technician with a limited understanding of the necessity to play in a team context. It was not that he lacked will, but that he misapplied it and had a tendency to lose concentration. Chelsea had paid nearly £7 million for him in the summer of 2003, but Cole could not persuade Claudio Ranieri to establish him in the team; he made half of his appearances for the Italian as a substitute. Mourinho, having cleared out some of Cole's competition in the creativity department – notably Juan Sebastián Verón – and been deprived of the unfortunate Scott Parker through injury, gave Cole some opportunities, but he soon lost his place to Damien Duff and in early October, after he had come off the bench to score the only goal of a home match with Liverpool, Mourinho alluded to the reasons: 'After he scored, the game finished for Joe. I need eleven players for defensive organisation and I had just ten. Joe had two faces – one beautiful and another which I did not like.'

Nearly six months later, Cole was picked to start a World Cup qualifying match against Northern Ireland at Old Trafford. England won 4–0 and Cole, having scored the first goal in some style, shaking off a challenge and sending a controlled drive into Maik Taylor's left-hand corner, performed with impressive maturity. 'He has finally learned,' said Sven-Göran Eriksson, 'that football is not about making tricks – it's about knowing when to do it. Today I don't think he ever lost the ball in a stupid position, which was his problem in the past. He showed he can beat people – you want him to do that – but also keep it simple, and he showed he can defend.' He had, in short, completed the journey from stage act to international footballer and Cole was not backward in thanking Mourinho. 'He's the first person to really look at me and my game,' declared Cole. 'I can genuinely say he's had a massive influence on my career. I listen to him – he's a European champion.' And the public admonition after the Liverpool match had had its effect. 'Something like that can ram the nail home and I know what I've got to do now. His criticism is always constructive. He'll always sit me down and talk about my game and what he wants me to do. He's so advanced with the tactical stuff and he's made me really think about that side of things. There's been a steady improvement and I can become even better.'

Deco was another beneficiary of Mourinho's guide to self-discovery. It occurred to me during the latter stages of Porto's successful Champions League run that here was a team so disciplined as to bear comparison with the Milan founded by Arrigo Sacchi or – the search for another example ended closer to home – George Graham's Arsenal. Just as those teams were leavened by highly creative players, Mourinho acknowledged the necessity for flair by having Deco as a key man. For all his gifts, though, Deco did not just wait for the ball to come to him; he worked and probed and challenged until the openings came. In short, he was – to use a favourite word of Graham's – productive. 'Mourinho is special,' Deco has said, 'because he is one of the few people capable of changing a player's mentality. He didn't change the way I play – he improved it. He got me thinking a lot more.' Deco, who was born and raised in Brazil, developed so well under Mourinho that he was encouraged to take Portuguese nationality. He made his debut for his adopted country shortly before the UEFA Cup final in 2003. It was at home against Brazil – and he scored the only goal. Much of Deco's life has resembled a fairy tale since; he even recovered from the disappointment of Barcelona's defeat at Chelsea to collect a Spanish championship at the climax of his first season at the Camp Nou.

Another player of talent was Abdelsatar Sabry, an Egyptian known simply as Sabry in Portugal. He was at Benfica when Mourinho arrived in September 2000 and popular with the fans. Although skilled and with a knack of scoring in big matches, Sabry had no sense of team play. He was like an unreformed Joe Cole, only more so. He objected to Mourinho's use of him on the left flank and, what was more, told a newspaper as much; he said he wanted a free role behind the main striker. Mourinho responded in public. He said Sabry kept giving the ball away and cited a derby against Belenenses in which he lost possession so often that, at one stage, Benfica were counter-attacked five times in sixteen minutes. 'A number-ten player,' Mourinho continued, referring to the playmaker's role, the Deco role, 'must display a high tactical level in order to be a link between the defence and attack – *but not the defence and attack of the opponent.*' As if this were not a devastating enough dismissal of Sabry's analysis of his own worth, Mourinho added that he was forever being caught offside. Oh, and he wasn't scoring enough goals. As events were to transpire, Mourinho went and Sabry stayed, at least for a while. Two years later, when Mourinho was at Porto and a burgeoning Deco about to take the international stage, Sabry was at Estrela da Amadora, with little to celebrate but the favourable verdict of a court on his demand that Benfica stump up more than £200,000 in unpaid wages.

Mourinho has never been interested in players who are reluctant to learn and the quality of those he coaches at Chelsea has helped to produce swift results. Even in the Carling Cup final, one of his beliefs was effectively enacted. Earlier in the season, Scott Parker had alluded to it when he said: 'We are doing a lot more ball work, playing keep-ball.' This was to do with Mourinho's concept of 'resting on the ball', which he has described as 'keeping possession for the sake of possession' on the grounds that it is safer to rest when your team, rather than the opposition, have the ball. When he was at Porto, an opposing coach complimented Mourinho after a match by saying his players had never come off the field so tired. Chelsea used the ploy in making Liverpool chase for long periods in Cardiff and afterwards Terry said: 'We saw their legs go.' Against Barcelona in the Champions League, the work Chelsea do on both aspects of 'transitions' (counter-attacking) was manifest. Mourinho, asked by Andy Roxburgh which trends he had noticed in the contemporary game, replied: 'Transitions have become crucial. When the opponent is organised defensively, it is very difficult to score. The moment the opponent loses the ball can be the time to exploit the opportunity of someone being out of position. Similarly, when we lose the ball, we must react immediately. In training I sometimes practise keeping a minimum of five players behind the ball, so that when we lose it we can still keep a good defensive shape. The players must learn to read the game – when to press and when to get back to their defensive positions. Everybody says that set plays win most games, but I think it is more about transitions.'

Mourinho would appreciate something David Moyes said about Chelsea: 'They're a clever team.' The Everton coach was referring to the match between the clubs at Goodison Park in February, when Everton's James Beattie was sent off early for butting William Gallas. 'It was interesting,' said Moyes. 'We couldn't get the ball from them. They wouldn't let it out of play and they didn't concede free-kicks. We were doing everything we could to find a way of restarting the game with a throw or a corner or a free-kick so we could make it a scrap for the ball. With ten men, it would have been our best opportunity. They didn't give us it and I remember thinking what an intelligent team they were.' There was something else Mourinho did that day which Moyes, when I told him about it, thought clever. But it was more in the way of management than coaching, so we shall save it for a moment. They do, though, blend into each other, coaching and management.

Infectious, isn't it, this global spirit?

Management

That day at Everton had presented Mourinho with a problem. Chelsea had led the Premiership for three months – since they beat Everton at Stamford Bridge – and, although Arsenal had yet to recover the form their Old Trafford experience had disrupted, Manchester United were challenging. Chelsea went to Merseyside with a nine-point advantage. United had a derby against Manchester City the following day. The dismissal of James Beattie seemed just what Chelsea would have wanted, but breaching a depleted team is not always easy, as Mourinho told us. He was responding to someone who asked, before the trip to Barcelona, if it were not a comfort at such times to be sitting on a cushion at the top of one's domestic league. He smiled ruefully. 'Maybe you won't believe this,' he said, 'but towards the end of the first half at Everton, between the thirtieth and forty-fifth minutes, I felt the players were too anxious to score against ten men and lost their shape.' Having devised a means of relieving them of their obligation, he strode to the dressing room. 'I told them to let the game flow, because a point would be good, no problem. "If we drop two points," I said, "we stay seven points clear, even if Manchester United win tomorrow. So there's no pressure. Now let's go." I didn't make any changes. I didn't scream at them. I just reminded them of those nine points and said, "If we score, we score. If we don't score, we don't score." ' He paused slightly. '*I was desperate to score!*' Eidur Gudjohnsen obliged and Chelsea had three more points. United, though they won at the City of Manchester Stadium, realised – because that weekend, given the status Everton had acquired, had been seen as a milestone – they were fighting for second place. What did Moyes, now he had been apprised of Mourinho's team-talk, think of it? 'Great management.'

Management has always been to do with psychology. And Mourinho has never been above playing the odd trick on his own men. A few days before what turned out to be his last match with Benfica – the derby against Sporting – he decided to indulge his affection for tennis at the Masters Cup, which was being held in Lisbon that year. He went with his assistant, Carlos Mozer, and, having spotted the Sporting players strolling among the throng of spectators, resolved to turn this to his advantage. He told Mozer he was going to 'poison' his own team by telling them the Sporting players were obviously so confident of thrashing Benfica they had neglected to prepare for the match in favour of disporting themselves all week at the tennis. He was, of course, exaggerating wildly and later confessed to it; he had simply been spinning the tale in order to put an additional edge on his own players' appetites for the derby, which they won 3–0.

No slight, real or imagined, is ever wasted. Most coaches do this but few have done it as effectively as Mourinho. Sir Alex Ferguson is a great exponent. In the Scot's first big job, at Aberdeen, he used the city's relative isolation from Glasgow, where the 'Old Firm' of Rangers and Celtic had traditionally ruled the game, to build a stockade mentality, and he contrived to do much the same at Manchester United, even though the club was the best supported in the land; the players were led to believe that everyone, including those in authority in the game, was out to get them or at least desperate to see them fail. No wonder he and Mourinho clashed when they faced each other in the Champions League: they were two of a kind. Mourinho, once Chelsea had all but taken the English title, admitted to using similar tactics. Or almost admitted it. What he said was that there had been a 'psychological fight' against critics who had called his team 'boring' in the opening weeks of the season. 'Maybe the criticism made us stronger. We had to close the shell. We created something strong inside. We went through that period and then a beautiful period.' And, once on top, they had remained strong. 'We always look at newspapers and TV and every day there was a headline saying Chelsea will have a blip, Arsenal will come back, United will shock them, Chelsea will lose points in the north, Chelsea will lose points in the south. All season! We needed to be strong.' I imagined him staying up all night in the team hotel, prowling the corridors when the newspapers came round and carefully cutting out all the complimentary bits before they could read them and go weak at the knees.

The most unusual facet of Mourinho's management also pertains to his bonding technique. Scorning the convention that even the kindest coach must maintain a certain distance between himself and the players, he actually behaves like one of them, a sort of twelfth man. It has been especially noticeable since he came to Chelsea. He celebrated victory over Barcelona by running on to the pitch, roaring and wheeling his right arm, with the fist clenched, so that the tail of the famous grey overcoat fluttered; lest it be thought he had succumbed to total abandon, however, I should add that he kept a firmly restraining left hand on the pocket containing his mobile phone. Then Mourinho jumped player-style on the broad back of his captain, John Terry. It was that great observer of the human race (and inveterate football follower) Desmond Morris who drew my attention to it. 'I cannot think of another manager who could have got away with that,' he added. 'If Big Ron Atkinson had tried it, he'd probably have broken the poor lad's back!' But Morris had a point to make. 'Both of Mourinho's legs were off the ground. It was a piece of body language I've never seen in football before. It means he's one of the players.'

What's more, his participation in some of Chelsea's wildest celebrations seemed perfectly natural in the context of that particular man and those players. As Ian Wright put it: 'If another manager hugged his players, they might be sort-of rigid, cringing, embarrassed. But you can see the camaraderie between him and the team. There is a deep respect there. You can see that they really love him.'

Love?

I thought that might be a bit strong. So I decided to ask a less excitable, more seasoned footballing figure for his impression. 'No,' said Gérard Houllier, 'it's true. He has this kind of complicity with the players. They don't just like José. They love him.' And he loves them, as you can see from his post-match tours. And they love each other, which became increasingly apparent during the march to the title when kisses were commonly exchanged. In the match programme for the home leg of the Champions League tie against Liverpool there is a picture of Claude Makelele, his face obscured by the enveloping arms of Terry, who is leaning down and planting an earnest smacker on the top of his head; Makelele has his left arm wrapped tightly round the captain's waist. Players do that kind of thing. But usually they do it with a grin. Although at Mourinho's Chelsea some demonstrations of affection have flirted with the outer fringes of the faintly nauseating, they have, I confess, also stirred feelings of wonder at how it must be on the inside of such a passionate scrum, especially while everything is being carried before it. These players have been led to believe in each other and throughout the 2004–05 season, courtesy of Sky television's access to the pre-match tunnel, we could see Terry glance over his shoulder at colleagues who clearly shared his conviction that they could not lose. The central significance of Terry's relationship with Mourinho to the events of the season was undeniable and in March the captain declared: 'Every result is for the manager. He works so hard, him and his staff. On the pitch all of us fight for each other but deep down it's for him. He's the best, we believe he's the best and we're lucky to have him. Everything about the man is first class.'

Mourinho went about the job of unifying the Chelsea dressing room straight away. Cliques were out, he told the press quite bluntly: 'You go to some places and maybe you find an English corner, a French corner and, at some clubs, a black corner. I don't like any of that. It cannot work.' There would be a common language: 'If you are on my table for breakfast and I keep speaking Portuguese, you turn round and say, "Sorry, fuck off, I don't sit at your table any more." The language has to be English. If they don't speak it fluently when they come, they must study.' They soon discovered one reason why. Mourinho announced that the final team-talk before matches would be given not by him but by a player. Before the Bayern Munich matches, when Mourinho was suspended, the young German defender Robert Huth said: 'We have a meeting with him two hours before a game and after that everybody is left to themselves because we all have different ways to prepare. Then we go for the warm-up, but it's not like the coach has a big final word. He leaves it up to one of us to give the rallying call. We choose the player on the day.' By 'we' he means the players and staff: often Stevie Clarke makes the final decision.

Mourinho informed them they were unbeatable and should never forget it, because successful teams had no fear of losing. The allure of such meaningless statements, usually purloined from the writings of American sports coaches, escapes many outsiders, but it is rarely lost on players. Chelsea's were told that Porto had been fearless and that, given Porto's achievements, was good enough for them. When the Champions League pitted them against Barcelona, said Terry: 'Initially you think "great side", which they are, but when you've got a manager drumming it into you every day that you are the best, that there isn't going to be anybody better, it rubs off on the players and we go out there believing it.' Lampard added that Mourinho had the knack of being able to transmit his 'amazing confidence' to every player.

He has an almost quaint liking for pen and paper. Everything he has done in his coaching career, from day one with the youths at Vitória Setúbal, has been written in notebooks and retained. This is not unique. Everton's David Moyes told me: 'I've written down what every coach I've ever worked with has done – with my own ideas alongside, such as "I wouldn't have put the centre-half in here" or whatever. Even now, my assistant, Alan Irvine, writes down everything we do at Everton – I could tell you what our training routines were three years ago last Thursday! But José, as I say, somehow manages to make it sound sexy.' His habit of getting substitutes to carry on written messages to other players fascinated Portuguese viewers; the cameras would zoom in to try to sneak a look. He continued the habit in England and, after Jiří Jarošík had carried on written instructions for Tiago at Everton, the referees' overseer, Keith Hackett, was asked if regulations allowed it. 'Yes,' said an amused Hackett. 'There is nothing in the laws to prevent it. It might be different if the substitute took a Christmas hamper on to the pitch.' As always with Mourinho, however, these billets-doux have a serious purpose. Asked about the illustrated tutorial Dmitri Alenitchev was given before taking the field in Porto's Champions League final, Roxburgh said: 'José's clever enough to know which players can absorb words and which need to be shown things visually.'

To call him a hands-on coach would be understating it.

While serving one of his dugout bans in Portugal, where a suspended coach is allowed to speak to his players at half-time, he was stopped on a landing by a security guard at the stadium of Porto's local rivals, Boavista, but simply picked up his mobile phone; the players heard his reassuring voice on a speaker-phone one of his assistants had taken the precaution of carrying into the dressing room. When he was banned from the second leg of the UEFA Cup semi-final against Lazio in Rome, he texted messages to the bench. One translates as 'Tell Deco I'm pissed off – I want more', another as 'Pressure on linesman, everybody'. While the latter confirms Mourinho is a psychological warrior, it is almost standard coaching practice to order your players to chip away at match officials in the hope of obtaining a marginal decision sooner or later. What set him somewhat apart was his foray from the dugout physically to prevent the Lazio player Lucas Castromán from taking a quick throw in the UEFA Cup semi-final first leg (which Porto won 4–1). For that he incurred the suspension in Rome (there the match ended 0–0) and Roxburgh, recalling how hard it hit him, could not quite suppress a laugh. 'José came to one of our UEFA meetings some time later and it clearly still rankled. Not the red card. "I deserved that," he said. "The referee was absolutely right. I had no excuse for what I did." Because one thing all these guys are is brutally honest with themselves. But José went on to say it was an absolute disgrace that, as well as denying him a seat in the dugout, they would not let him in the dressing room at half-time. He was raging about it. A lot of the others – Fergie and Wenger and people like that – were listening and some were nodding and thinking maybe he had a point. And naturally coaches are going to think that. So I took it up with UEFA. But they think a banned coach should be banned from doing any coaching at a match.' While Mourinho might have seemed to have lost the argument, his antics during his next ban, over the two legs of Chelsea's encounter with Bayern, emphasised his reluctance to accept defeat.

Mourinho's handling of players has changed over the few short years of his solo career. While at Benfica there were Sabry, for whom fate had disappointment in store, and Maniche, who played up in training, was banished to the reserves but two weeks later became club captain and ended up one of Mourinho's European champions at Porto, you hardly ever hear the crack of a whip around Chelsea's training ground, at least not on the players' backs. There, the boss is almost one of the lads. While they are lacing their boots, he tells funny stories of occurrences in his career, much as a player would. When he has to be tough, he will be, as in the case of Adrian Mutu, but the distance another coach would keep between himself and his charges is not observed. On the field, it is a similar story and, when they celebrate at the end of a match, a stranger would be able to tell him from

Tiago and the others only through the realisation that an on-duty player would not be wearing a cashmere coat.

According to Desmond Morris, the phenomenon is linked to football's evolution. Morris and football go back a long way. The author of *The Naked Ape*, *The Human Zoo* and a dozen other popular studies of man and other animals, he has been watching the game for nearly seventy years and was a director of Oxford United during their rise (funded by Robert Maxwell) to the top division in the eighties. 'There was a time,' he said, 'when the captain was an important figure. In modern football, his role has become all but non-existent and the manager has taken over, leading the team and connecting it to the public through television, radio and other media, generally representing it. The manager has become a performer and the good manager will always support his team. Mourinho, though, identifies with his team more than any other manager. He is passionately involved with them. In his imagination, he is out there with them. He really is the twelfth man. As for keeping a distance, he doesn't feel a need to do it. He gets on the pitch and celebrates with them and that is what makes him different. You couldn't envisage Alex Ferguson jumping on a player's back. Or Arsène Wenger. That's why I disagree slightly with the portrayal of Mourinho as a father figure to his players. He is more like an elder brother. Or the leader of the gang.'

There is, nevertheless, an element of awe in the

players' perception of Mourinho. 'He jokes with every-one,' said Frank Lampard, 'but at the same time you're a little bit wary of him.' Perhaps they sense what Roxburgh has always discerned behind his charismatic façade: a willingness to make ruthless decisions. 'It's one of the elements of management,' said Roxburgh. 'Fergie has always had it. He can like you as a person but make a decision that hurts you.' In Ferguson's case, the mind usually travels back in time to the dropping of Jim Leighton, who, after keeping goal more than reliably for Aberdeen throughout their greatest years, followed Ferguson to Manchester United and, having performed unconvincingly in the 1990 FA Cup final against Crystal Palace, a 3–3 draw, lost his place for the replay five days later; United won 1–0 and Leighton's career was never quite the same again. Mourinho, too, could separate his human feelings from the cause of the team, said Roxburgh, and we could expect to see that if anyone repeated Adrian Mutu's error in letting him down. Might this ruthlessness, also evident in the rapid rebuilding of Porto, have been picked up from Louis van Gaal, the man who dropped Rivaldo? 'It's intrinsic,' said Roxburgh. 'It might have been lent emphasis by the time he spent with Louis, but I think it was already there inside him.'

The most exciting part of management calls for tough decisions to be made very quickly. It is the bit we see: the match. Sir Bobby Robson has a story about that and he told it at one of Roxburgh's UEFA gatherings. 'It was in

Barcelona several years ago,' said Roxburgh. 'We had our fifty-two coaches from fifty-two countries and Bobby was giving a lecture on crisis management. He was talking about a time when his Barcelona side were getting whacked 3–0 at home and the white hankies were up and the whole bit. We were showing clips from the game as the goals went in and saying, "What were you thinking now, Bobby?" and Bobby replied, "At that point, I was thinking about a taxi." And then, having pulled two goals back early in the second half, they let in another. When we asked Bobby what he was thinking then, I remember Rinus Michels in the front row shouting, "Get that taxi!" And yet Barcelona won the game. José was beside Bobby in the dugout and I thought back to it when I watched José send on three substitutes at half-time when Chelsea were losing at Newcastle in the FA Cup.' So did Robson.

Let him take up the tale of that Barcelona match. 'It was against Atlético Madrid in the Cup and that, in Spain, means war. The capital against Catalunya. Whether it's Real or Atlético, it matters to our crowd. So when we go 3–0 down the hankies start fluttering. I nudged my assistant. "José," I said. "It's snowing." I had a look across the pitch and formed an idea. I didn't like the way Laurent Blanc was playing and I didn't think much of Gica Popescu either. So both of those central defenders were candidates to come off. I thought I'd do that – even though Popescu was our captain and there were still several minutes to go to the interval – and replace them with attacking players, people who might get us goals. After all, what did we have to lose? The only way we could save the game was by going forward.' A measure of defensive capability would still be provided by Abelardo, Sergi and Fernando Couto. 'I remember telling José what I was going to do and asking what he thought about it. "You've got no option, Mister," he replied. "Do it." ' Blanc and Popescu were called to the bench together and Hristo Stoichkov and Juan Antonio Pizzi took the field. Within five minutes of the resumption, Ronaldo and Iván de la Peña had struck. Atlético's Milinko Pantic retaliated by completing his hat-trick. 'A bloody soft goal,' said Robson, recalling a blunder by his Portuguese goal-keeper, Vítor Baía, who was later to become a European champion under Mourinho at Porto. 'Anyway, that's us 4–2 down. Then we scored three! Figo, Ronaldo and finally Pizzi. So we won 5–4. And we were still going like pistons at the end. Another twenty minutes and we'd have won 8–4. There were some stunning shots.'

Robson's message to his fellow coaches at the UEFA gathering, said Roxburgh, was twofold: 'Keep calm – and always give the other coach a problem. Don't just send on a big striker for another big striker. Change it. Give your opponent things to think about. I've seen Bobby make other triple substitutions that have come off. That's why what José did at Newcastle in the FA Cup was interesting – even though it was probably too big a gamble. I think he gleaned a lot about management from Bobby.'

Robson, asked if the merit of being bold with your substitutions might have been one lesson that was absorbed, replied: 'I hope so. Mind you, I don't think he will ever again, as long as he lives, change all three at half-time when the score is tight. You do that when you're losing 3–0 at half-time and stuffed anyway. The thing to do is change two and hold one in reserve – then maybe stick him on with twenty minutes to go. Yes, I have made triple substitutions. I went to Liverpool a few years ago and sent three on when we were 3–1 down with twenty minutes to go. We drew 3–3. Even twenty minutes from the end it's a gamble. But forty-five minutes is too long, as José discovered. He was a little too bold that day, a little too confident in himself.'

Mind games:
the fourth hat?

At the height of the controversy over José Mourinho's reaction to the first-leg defeat Chelsea sustained in Barcelona and the subsequent retirement of the match referee, Anders Frisk, a few people suggested that I obtain a videotape of some of Mourinho's appearances at press conferences and take it to a psychologist. So I consulted a friend of a friend who happens to be a psychoanalyst. He said it would be a waste of time: 'You have to bear in mind that almost every conversation Mourinho has is part of his work, and that the ultimate purpose of each of these communications is not to communicate as such but to increase his team's chances of winning. In a press conference, he is not talking to the people in the room so much as those beyond – his players, other managers, the FA and so on. The advice I would give is the sporting equivalent of what every political interviewer should constantly be asking themselves: "Why is this lying bastard lying to me?" '

Mourinho has couched it in language which would get past the Speaker of the House of Commons. 'Talking to the media is part of the game,' he has said. 'When I go to a press conference before a game, in my mind the game has already started. When I go to a press conference after the game, the game hasn't finished yet. Or, if the game has finished, the next one has already started.' He has also said both he and Sir Alex Ferguson like these mind games and they certainly seem no more able to resist them than the player who is unable to keep his tugging hands off a passing opponent's shirt. Indeed Mourinho, Ferguson and Arsène Wenger, the Premiership's leading trio of coaches, appear as hopelessly addicted to the mind-game habit as stormbound gamblers betting on which of two raindrops rolling down the outside of a window will be the first to reach the sill. Whichever metaphor you choose, it is the competitive instinct at work. Plus, perhaps, an element of ego in the case of Mourinho, whose maintenance of contact with his homeland through frequent appearances in the Portuguese media cannot be explained by the frequently aired theory that the publicity he attracts takes pressure off his players.

It is not as if he is consistent. In November 2004, after Wenger had done a Ferguson and ranted at a fourth official during a Champions League match in Eindhoven, a soft-focus Mourinho sought to portray himself as the match officials' friend, saying: 'I feel like an angel when I see how other managers behave in relation to referees and fourth officials. I let these people do their work and get on with mine.' To the protestation that he had been involved in several rows with referees in Portugal, he responded that he had become calmer since moving to England. This struck me as very clever: the kind of thing that, one day down the line, might earn Chelsea a marginal decision. And rather nice too, a most welcome note of calm sanity amid the turbulence of the English game. A couple of months later, however, Mourinho was insulting Frisk and being escorted down the Cardiff tunnel. Some angel.

The suspicion is that Mourinho simply enjoys the sound of his voice, especially when it is being mischievous. Few Chelsea players would have disagreed with Deco, who burgeoned under Mourinho at Porto, when he said: 'In the dressing room Mourinho is quite relaxed, but when he gets talking to the press he likes to wind things up – he is playing a role.' But he does know when to stay quiet in his team's interests, unlike the more experienced Ferguson, whose head-to-head record in mind games against Mourinho is unimpressive. When Manchester United went to play Porto, the pair clashed in the technical area, Ferguson angrily complaining to Mourinho (so the fourth official could hear) about his players' perceived exaggeration of the impact of tackles.

Ferguson kept up the campaign in the press before the second leg, and one or two United players weighed in with some taunts along the lines that their adversaries had been girlish. It was a little unpleasant. Yet, after it had backfired, both Ferguson and Gary Neville were quick to knock on Porto's dressing-room door and wish them all the best in the next round.

Ferguson would, I suppose, have to be granted a place in any mind-game hall of fame, if only for his past contributions. He may even have helped to define the art with his demand that Leeds United try their damnedest against Newcastle towards the end of the 1995–96 season, when Kevin Keegan's team were being challenged for the title by Ferguson's. Keegan, interviewed by Sky while wearing headphones – never an aid to a man's dignity – exuded indignation as he declared how he would 'love it, really love it, if we beat them' and was widely believed to have unsettled his own players at that moment. United came from a long way behind to take the title and, ever since, the words of the managers have constituted a large proportion, perhaps inordinately so, of the media's coverage of Premiership football. But Ferguson, when he had another chip at Mourinho last season, again came off second best. He said Chelsea might struggle when they had to travel to the north. True, they had lost at Manchester City – where Keegan was in charge – but once Ferguson's jibe had been brought to their attention they took full points at Everton, Liverpool and Blackburn before clinching the title at Bolton. And then they won at Manchester United when they didn't need to.

Yet he and Ferguson get on well personally. 'I respect Sir Alex,' Mourinho has said, 'but not just respect – I like him. He is a person to fight with but a person who, when the game ends, I can share a glass of wine with and speak openly.' A sign that Ferguson reciprocates those feelings is that he has poked fun at Mourinho through the press, accusing him of offering 'some cheap Portuguese plonk' when United went to Stamford Bridge. Mind games could be seen as hard banter in that neither side wishes to lose face. But every coach to whom you speak insists that they have a serious purpose. 'He wants to protect his players,' said Louis van Gaal. 'I am certain of that. I do it. And I find it logical that a coach should look for a way of helping his team to win the game. You can condition the environment for your players. Maybe he went too far in Barcelona, but later it came out that Frank Rijkaard *had* spoken to the referee, so there was an element of truth in what Mourinho said.'

An element. But surely he was still wrong to accuse Frisk of favouring Barcelona? 'Yes,' said Van Gaal, 'but a lot of coaches have said a referee's decision was wrong and been vindicated by television. I think the referee is always the main influence in a game. Mourinho got emotionally involved, because he is an emotional man – he always was, and now he can show it – and maybe he regrets the business with Frisk, but he cannot rewind the tape and wipe out what happened, so he has to go on. Such are the errors a coach makes at the beginning of his career.' We cannot say with any certainty that Mourinho's Barcelona antics worked for his team in the Champions League, but it is a fact that they eventually ousted Barcelona with a goal that should not have been allowed. As for the questionable goal-line decision that Mourinho claimed went against them at Anfield, it may actually have worked in their favour. That is on the assumption that the referee would otherwise have awarded a penalty and dismissed Petr Čech.

What we can safely assert is that Mourinho will not stop playing these games. They are not prerequisites of footballing achievement; Rafael Benítez did not indulge in them before Liverpool knocked Chelsea out of the Champions League or won the final. In Istanbul, on the morning after Liverpool had completed one of the most amazing European triumphs by recovering from a 3–0 deficit to beat Milan on penalties, I asked Benítez why he scorned these little ploys. He smiled and replied: 'Maybe my English is not good enough at the moment.' So he had done it in the past, with Valencia? 'No. I prefer to concentrate on working with my team. It is more important.' Nor did Luiz Felipe Scolari feel the need to play mind games while steering Brazil to success in the World Cup. Nor Otto Rehhagel during Greece's European Championship triumph. They are just part of Mourinho's style and, given what he has won thus far, are likely to become increasingly fashionable. To quote Desmond Morris: 'The manager has become a performer and the good manager will always support his team.' So the handsome young twelfth man of Chelsea will toy with the minds of opponents and referees and every other form of authority for as long as they let him get away with it. To the minds of many people, what Mourinho said about Frisk was unacceptably impudent. Yet again some words of Machiavelli are apposite: 'Fortune, like a woman, is friendly to the young, because they show her less respect, they are more daring and command her with audacity.'

PART FOUR

Behind the mask

Humourless?
You're having a laugh

A stranger arriving at Chelsea's training ground might never guess that the dark and handsome man in the tracksuit was the boss. Mostly José Mourinho just goes about his business deep in thought. Beneath the placid surface, however, is a volatile temper that keeps people on their toes. Everyone knows the seriousness with which he takes matters of detail and, when he feels the heads of subordinate departments have not matched it, loud bellowing may be heard from the unfortunate's office. Neil Frazer, the doctor who left a few months after Mourinho's arrival, suffered on several occasions, notably when the wrong X-rays of Arjen Robben were produced. It can happen during matches too. Towards the end of a robust affair at Blackburn, the midfielder Tiago was called off and, when he came to the bench, the staff were not able to provide one of the replenishments required for a substituted player: it might have been a drink, or a tablet.

Mourinho exploded and within seconds the physiothera-pist, Mike Banks, was sprinting down the tunnel to the dressing room to fetch the missing item.

In consequence, things rarely go wrong and Mourin-ho's behaviour is polite and charming, if brisk; he hates to waste time. People are told what he wants and it is done. Very little happens without his being consulted, even if its link with the football side of the operation is tenuous. This is relatively new to him, this broad English view of the job, and, although it has led to the odd tense moment with the chief executive, Peter Kenyon, he rather likes it. But he is happiest among the players and, when they come in for training, the boss becomes a bit of a lad. He joins them as they put their kit on and tells tales that make them smile. When they poke merciless fun at the masseur, Billy McCulloch – every dressing room has someone who serves as the butt of jokes – Mourinho joins in the laughter. It would be hard to imagine Sir Alex Ferguson doing that, let alone Arsène Wenger or Rafael Benítez. Or indeed the late Brian Clough. Yet in the early stages of Mourinho's time in England, and especially the aftermath of Clough's death, a frequent criticism of the newcomer was that he lacked a sense of humour.

Alan Hansen, once the most elegant of defenders with Liverpool and now a *Daily Telegraph* columnist, put it thus after Mourinho had complained that Tottenham had 'parked their bus' (played too defensively) at Stamford Bridge: 'When Clough talked his mind – and I certainly never agreed with him all the time – he did so with one important quality in evidence. He was funny. Mourinho, for all his colourful opinions, is never funny. And we all know how hard it is to like someone who seems to lack a sense of humour.' I suppose it depends how you define a sense of humour, but, if it involves a readiness to smile, even when the figure of gentle fun is yourself, Mourinho could hardly be found deficient. On the day he was banned from the dugout at Boavista, and Porto won 1–0 under the notional control of his assistant Baltemar Brito, he rang his players at half-time on the speaker-phone that had been smuggled into the dressing room, and told them: 'I'm stuffed. You're beating Boavista 1–0 and Brito is twisting the knife. After the game I'll be unemployed.' The players immediately began chanting, 'Brito is the greatest.' Mourinho clearly relished that for he told the story in his book. He took the joke, too, when Liverpool fans at Stamford Bridge told him to 'Shush' and, the day before, he had been in sparkling form with the press. 'When I arrived here last summer,' he said, stretching his arms wide, 'my ego was this big.' Had it got smaller? He grinned. 'No, it's even bigger!' This brought the house down, but, while his chum Ferguson has noted 'a wit and humour about him', a lot of the laughs he coaxes from us are derived from his aura as much as any special comic gift; he gets laughs like royalty. When Sir Bobby Robson was told about Hansen's first impression of Mourinho, he replied: 'Well, I can see what he means. José was sober and serious a lot of the time. But there was plenty of the banter with the players and, as for me, I just thought he was a good lad to be around. I wouldn't like to say he had no sense of humour.' Maybe he just suffers, in this respect, from comparison with Clough, the home-bred iconoclast. As Desmond Morris told me: 'Because Cloughie could be outrageous with a nod and a wink, people weren't as offended as they might have been. He had this northern humour and used it as the sugar coating on the pill of his rudeness.'

But this is only the Mourinho we see. The person who knows him better than anyone, his wife Matilde – 'Tami', as he calls her – has spoken of the mask that often covers his feelings and how she can discern them through a gesture or a look. Mourinho's father was always like that. A friend of the family told me Félix was 'like an electric kettle – on the outside, smooth and steady, but inside boiling'. Mourinho's mother was 'a fighter'. So he has characteristics of both parents. But he is also very much a self-made personality with the knack of being able to separate his private life, such as it has become since he left Portugal, from work. 'I don't like to say that I'm a man with two faces,' he told his audience at the Peres Center in Tel Aviv, 'but José Mourinho the manager and the man are very different. It's important to separate them and I do that very easily.'

The man was seventeen when he found his woman. She was fourteen. They met at a teenage disco in Setúbal, where Matilde's family had landed after fleeing the newly independent Angola five years earlier; her father had served in the Portuguese forces. Nine years after their meeting, when José was teaching PE and, fortified by the course he had attended in Scotland the previous summer, coaching the Vitória youths, they were wed. Matilde, having graduated from the Catholic University of Lisbon with a degree in philosophy, was soon introduced to the nomadic existence of a football man's wife. First there was the dead-end year with Manuel Fernandes at Estrela da Amadora and then the open road, the times with Robson at Sporting Lisbon, Porto and Barcelona, where the Mourinhos' first child, a girl, was born. They gave her the name Matilde but, in order to avoid confusion, called her 'Tita'. Four years later, their son was born. He got Mourinho's forenames, José Mário, so the infant needed a nickname too and was given 'Zuca'. Until around the time of the Portuguese revolution, it was almost compulsory for parents to hand their first names on to the eldest son and daughter. Today it is seen by many as an irritating anachronism, good for little else than the maintenance of the silly-nickname industry, and remains popular only among aristocratic or conservative families.

José Mourinho is of the latter tradition. Although his goalkeeper father was of relatively humble birth, marriage introduced Félix to the advantages of association with fascist Portugal's ruling class and, given the love and attention that surrounded José as he grew up, he could almost be described as the product of an over-privileged background; at least he did not have to fight his way out of the *favela*, the *barrio* or the ghetto, or leave a remote village at a tender age, like some of those who have acquired fame and fortune through professional sport. But he has neither been given nor asked for an easy ride. The Portuguese, to generalise, are often quite passive people, so much so that in such fields as marketing and the media today many key positions in the country have been occupied by Brazilians; in 2004 the trend even manifested itself in football when Portugal hosted the European Championship and the Brazilian Scolari was in charge of their team. The phenomenon is known as 'reverse colonisation'. It does not affect Mourinho. No territory of his is ever negotiable. Yet he nurses the chip on the shoulder that reminds us of his nationality. No wonder he fitted in so well among those Scots at Largs. Because, just as Scotland sometimes feels obscured by England, Portugal lives in the shadow cast by Spain. Or thinks it does.

Mourinho says his friends laugh when he is called arrogant. It does not surprise me because, when you walk in his footsteps, you are liable to hear only the opposite. There was the story told by Tosh McKinlay about Mourinho's warm greeting in Glasgow after three years. Not long after I heard this, I happened to be in Lisbon for a UEFA Cup match between Sporting and Newcastle and met Mourinho's former pupil André Chin, who, having returned to Portugal many years after his family's emigration to Canada, was working at the hotel where I stayed. 'I saw Mourinho not so long ago,' he said, 'when he was coach of Porto, around the middle of the season when they won the Champions League. I went to buy some fried chicken in this place near our house in Setúbal and there he was. He looked at me and I recognised him. I held out my hand and asked if he remembered me and then it dawned on him. "André Chin," he said. "How long is it?" I said it had been sixteen or seventeen years. "My God," he said, "that's a long time. What have you been doing?" He always showed an interest in people. We spoke for about fifteen minutes and then he left. He's a great guy and deserves all the success he gets.'

A similar conclusion was reached by Ian Ross, director of communications at Everton Football Club, former journalist, long-standing friend of mine and, by his own admission, 'cynical old bastard'. He told me that, in his four years at Goodison Park, no one had made such an impact as Mourinho. 'The habit here,' Ross explained, 'is that the visiting manager wanders around the tunnel and dressing-room area, keeping himself to himself and having next to no contact with our staff. There are exceptions – Arsène Wenger, for example, who, if there's a lunchtime game on, comes up and very politely asks if he can watch it on television in the press room. People appreciate his good manners. Mourinho just shuffled around with his hands in the pockets of his famous overcoat, greeting everyone and saying how welcome he'd been made and how he'd heard a lot about Everton. And I don't just mean executives of the club. I mean he spoke to stewards and ball-boys as well. Sometimes people are in awe of the likes of Mourinho – but he was going up to them! The word spread around the club and, by the time he'd left, there was a sort of euphoric atmosphere around the place, as if it were a shopping mall that David Beckham had just been through. But it wasn't just his charisma. Mourinho had actually taken time out to have a laugh with people and make jokes about our battle with Liverpool for fourth place. He was full of respect for the history of the club, and for David Moyes as a coach. Now I am a cynical old bastard, but I value courtesy above all else and it didn't matter to Mourinho that he was speaking to people who had next to nothing compared with him. He was completely at his ease – and made sure they were. Like Wenger, he always introduced himself by name. He was, quite literally, unassuming. He lit the whole place up.'

Moyes didn't find him arrogant either. 'We had a drink and a chat down at Chelsea,' said the Everton coach, 'and I think the persona he puts over may be for the media. I suspect that behind it he's got the same fear of failure most of us have. It's what probably drives him. At our place, he didn't come in for a drink, funnily enough. He'd come up to me on the bench and shaken my hand when there were still two minutes to play. He'd been criticised a couple of weeks before for not shaking Mark Hughes's hand at Blackburn and I think the gesture to me was his way of saying, "I understand what you do in this country and I respect it. I'm not sure where it fits in my list of priorities. I'm maybe more interested in going to shake my own players' hands than the opposition manager's." I can't be sure. I may be off the mark there. But I think that, when he incurred a lot of the criticism, he was still finding his feet in a new country.'

There could be no more telling testimonial to a Chelsea coach than one from a Fulham supporter. It was at Craven Cottage, Fulham's attractive riverside home, that I was approached by Ian Aitken, who acts as match-day steward in the press room. 'The first time Mourinho came here,' said Aitken, 'we were walking along the touchline from the dressing rooms so he could be taken in to face the press – it's part of my job to escort the visiting manager – when he suddenly looked across the pitch and said he loved the stadium. "Of course you do," I said. "You've just won 4–1." And he said, "No, I've always loved this place – it's so old and traditional." I presumed he knew it through the Bobby Robson connection [Robson both played for and managed Fulham]. Then, when they came back in the Carling Cup, I was expecting him to talk about the game. And he suddenly asked if I'd seen the film *The Incredibles*. I said I hadn't and he told me it was marvellous. For a lifelong

Fulham supporter to like the Chelsea manager is unusual, but I found him delightful – charming.'

Sir Bobby Robson recalled Mourinho having an affection for the cinema: 'He'd talk of little but football. Except films. He loved them. I remember him once coming to me and saying, "Mister, I saw a great movie last night. You must go and see it. It was *Forrest Gump*." ' A film or meal with his wife is Mourinho's idea of a night out. He seldom drinks. When away, he relaxes by watching films on his laptop or reading. Last winter, asked which book he had on the go, he named the autobiography of the Colombian Nobel Prize-winner Gabriel García Márquez. He reads the occasional novel. His books are usually recommended by Matilde, an insatiable consumer of literature. She also bought his grey cashmere coat; it came from Armani, cost £1,200 and, at the end of a season during which it came to symbolise Chelsea's success, Mourinho announced that it was to be auctioned in aid of a children's cancer charity with which the club had become associated. José – or 'Zé Mário', as he is affectionately called – 'Tami', 'Tita' and 'Zuca' lived amid the stuccoed splendour of Eaton Square in Belgravia for their first year in London, before finding a home close to Chelsea's training ground in Surrey. They still cherish their other home in Setúbal, a fine edifice in its own right. Friends say they are unlikely ever to abandon José's roots, the place where he encountered so much pleasure and one particularly tragic episode of pain: he was called back from Barcelona for the death through septicaemia of his sister Teresa, a diabetic who had never recovered from the break-up of her marriage some years before and suffered from a distressing variety of problems. Except to those closest to him, Mourinho never spoke about it: the mask descended. 'I think she was always a worry for him,' said a friend.

Teresa, before her health failed, had been vivacious and extremely pretty. Looks ran in the family and José's have undoubtedly contributed to his success; not just his fame and sex-symbol status but his effectiveness as a coach. 'People in football hardly mention this,' said Desmond Morris, 'but he is an incredibly handsome man, film-star handsome, and it's the combination of that and his behaviour which really works. If he were an ugly little man, his style wouldn't be as effective.' Mainly because players are only too eager to accept him as one of them; they respect him all the more because of his attractiveness to women. It is not so much necessary for any coach as specifically helpful to this one. He is cool. 'If you were to cast someone to play him in a movie,' said Morris, 'it would have to be James Dean.' Indeed; for he is dark and brooding and redolent of youth culture. The youth culture of this or any other age.

Although Mourinho has said his life is a typical Portuguese combination of the three Fs – Family, Football and Fatima (religion) – and has stressed that he keeps the work in a separate compartment, there does seem to be an element of narcissism about him that makes the limelight-hogging a labour of love. In other words, it must come from within and cannot be explained away by the assertion that a lot of nice actors play villains. But so what? He entertains us and has hurt no one. Except our old friend Anders Frisk. Even that unalloyed fan Desmond Morris could not talk Mourinho out of this one: 'It was something he very much wanted to hear [the report by two Chelsea staff members that the Barcelona coach had been in the referee's room] and so he adopted it. In the heat of the moment, he made the mistake of saying he had seen it when he hadn't. The whole thing then became a bad smell and he didn't want to know about it.' But then, you may recall, he made his tasteless joke on Portuguese television about being unable to discuss the performance of a Portuguese referee in case he quit: a joke that tended to vindicate those ambivalent towards Mourinho's status as a wit.

So that surge of power that Robson talked about, that licence to insult that distinction in sport affords, had carried Mourinho over the line once or twice. But it did not make him a bad person.

Different class

Now a guessing game. See how many clues you need. Our man is a bright and ambitious coach who came to England in the summer of 2004 having just won European silverware. He joined one of the Premiership's biggest clubs and, upon being introduced to the squad, laid down some principles. He insisted the players must behave as a unit on and off the field. They must eat together, for instance, and stay at the table until the last man has finished, in order to prevent the formation of cliques. He said no player could place himself above the team or act like a star. 'The team,' he declared, 'is the star.' Having followed these instructions, they had a dramatically successful first season under his command. His name is Rafael Benítez. But it might have been José Mourinho, because most coaches espouse the same notions, by and large. Few, so far as I am aware, encourage their players to develop laziness, selfish individualism or wilful disobedience.

The differences between them are matters of emphasis or personality and these might be connected with each other. Take the respective attitudes of Benítez and Mourinho towards mind games: disdain in one case, keen relish in the other. So naturally the past managers with whom Mourinho has been compared are the larger-than-life characters, above all Brian Clough. Yet, according to one of Clough's key players at Nottingham Forest, their ways of going about the job could scarcely be more contrasting. Frank Clark was brought to Nottingham almost as soon as Clough arrived, from Newcastle, where he had been captain. He was thirty-one and dropping a division and could not even have dreamed he would be a European champion when his career ended in a haze of champagne four years later. But it happened. Forest were promoted in his second season, champions of England the next season and champions of Europe the season after that. They were to retain the European title, too, after Clark had retired and been replaced by Frank Gray. In the league table of footballing fairy tales, then, Clough's Forest will always stand above even Mourinho's Porto.

The decades which separate the careers of Clough and Mourinho are partly responsible for the contrast. 'Mourinho obviously studies the opposition in great detail,' said Clark. 'He spends hour after hour preparing his team for their next opponents, if necessary changing tactics from game to game. Brian hardly considered the opposition. He used just to tell us to play our game, a simple 4–4–2, because that was what we knew best. A lot more thought goes into the game today. But Brian, if he were around now, would probably be sticking to his philosophy.' Yet Clough was utterly unorthodox in other respects. Could you imagine Mourinho ordering the coach driver to pull off the M62 on the way to Liverpool and having him unload crates of beer intended for the post-match celebration? Then inviting his players to have a couple of drinks just a few hours before the kick-off? Yet Clough did that. Forest, 2–0 up from the home leg of their European Champions' Cup first-round tie against the holders, came away with a scoreless draw that night and went on to beat Malmö in the final. 'You had to be something truly special to get away with such ways of managing people,' said Clark, 'and Brian was, quite simply, a genius. There is, though, something of Brian in Mourinho's personality: the total belief in what he's doing and the fact that he's not afraid to voice an opinion.'

Few, since Clough, have made such an astonishing impact on the European game as Mourinho. Within two and a half years of going solo, he had won the UEFA Cup and a year later his Porto were champions of the continent. Clough rose swiftly enough. But he had six years at Derby, where he also won the domestic title and guided his side to the Champions' Cup semi-finals (they lost to Juventus), before working his miracles at Nottingham. In terms of triumphant entrances to the top-level coaching scene, it is hard to find challengers for Mourinho. One would be Fabio Capello, whose Milan secured the Italian title in each of his first three years and celebrated the hat-trick with a quite magnificent Champions League final victory over Barcelona in 1994. But there are not too many other candidates. Rafael Benítez is one of the few – in four seasons he has won the Spanish title twice and the UEFA Cup with Valencia and the Champions League with Liverpool – but at least the Spaniard had an apprenticeship. It remains to be seen whether Mourinho, or Benítez for that matter, can emulate Capello in maintaining their standards for fifteen years; he craftily steered Juventus past Milan to take the Italian title in 2004–05. But in Mourinho's case you can be sure we shall hear plenty about it if he does.

The 250 Israeli and Palestinian coaches who took diligent notes of his ninety-five-minute lecture in Tel Aviv in February 2005 might, however, have been wasting their time, in the sense that only Mourinho can make his methods work like they do: while words such as 'faith' and 'unity' are easy enough to say, they are difficult to translate into medals. Only the special ones can make their players grow.

Few men in English football have observed more than Peter Robinson, who, in over thirty-five years as secretary, chief executive and finally vice-chairman of Liverpool, shared in just about every form of triumph the English and European games have to offer. When Robinson joined the club in 1965, the manager was Bill Shankly, a Scot with cropped hair and a fanatical devotion to his team. 'Bill was probably as close as anyone to Mourinho in style,' Robinson told me, 'and yet he was completely different in one way. He was never boastful about himself. Only about his players. He would never have said *he* was a European champion. He would have said his players were. But Mourinho has the same talent for inspiration. Bill could certainly convince the players they were better than they were. By sheer enthusiasm and presence, he could make them feel superior, even though they knew in their hearts they were not. Intelligent lads like Brian Hall used to speak about it in tones of wonder for years afterwards. They were bewitched. That's probably the best word for it.' When Shankly came to Anfield from Huddersfield in December 1959, Liverpool were languishing in the second division. By the time he retired in 1974, they had won the English title on three occasions, the FA Cup twice and the UEFA Cup – and a platform had been built on which four European Champions' Cups were to be placed by Bob Paisley and Joe Fagan's sides in the space of eight years.

During much of Shankly's success, the captain was Emlyn Hughes, whom he not so much requested as demanded the board buy from Blackpool. 'I've never known Bill so insistent on having a player,' said

Robinson. 'Shankly adored Emlyn and Emlyn adored him and that seems to be the case with Mourinho and John Terry at Chelsea. The manager's drive is always carried on to the field.' How it is instilled in the players is more difficult to define, but Robinson agreed that a film-star presence was another common factor between Mourinho and Shankly. 'Bill, with his haircut and the way he wore his clothes, did have an air of James Cagney, who was still prominent on the screen in those days,' said Robinson, 'though the respect in which his players held him was mainly due to his knowledge of football and one hundred per cent devotion to it.'

Desmond Morris recalled Shankly: 'He wasn't particularly handsome, but he was charismatic. I met Bob Paisley once at Anfield – and he might have been the chap who looked after the boots. But Shankly had an extraordinary presence. Similar to Mourinho's. If you asked me who would be in the same category as Mourinho, I'd say Shankly and Clough. He has Clough's unpredictability.' Although Clough had a singular way of addressing people – 'he called them "young man", regardless of their age, in order to establish seniority' – Mourinho, too, could hold our attention. 'You hang on his words. He says things which are relevant and thought-provoking. He avoids clichés. He hasn't fallen into the slovenly "at the end of the day, that's what it's all about" mentality. He doesn't reach for a hackneyed phrase to get him off the hook. When Mourinho is asked a question, he thinks about the answer. Other managers have made an impression on the country over the years – not just Clough but Tommy Docherty and more recently Alex Ferguson – but I find myself watching all Chelsea matches now, just because of him. After one away match last season, he ordered the players to throw their shirts in the visiting fans' section. He just put a hand on his chest and jiggled his coat – obviously he'd told them to do it in advance and was reminding them. He's always coming up with something new – and surprises are attractive.'

One surprise was his professed adherence to a trait associated with Shankly: in the middle of last season, while Arjen Robben was out of action, he declared that he gave no thought to injured players. 'I don't want to think about Arjen Robben,' he said. 'I really don't. I think the best way to face an injury to a very important player is to forget him. I don't speak with him. He is in the medical department. When they tell me he is ready to start work with the technical staff, even if he is not a hundred per cent, we shall welcome him with open arms. When my fitness coach says he is ready to play, I will jump for joy. But at the moment I don't want to think about him. I have to support and motivate the others and I would never offer Arjen Robben as an excuse for something. We have the players and we want to work with them.' Shankly worked on the same principles and, although his cold-shouldering of casualties could appear almost heartless – he could hardly look them in the eye –

the morale of those available to the cause as their deputies was considered the priority. It was seldom found wanting.

The mind games played with referees or rivals in Shankly's time were never as hard-edged as Mourinho's – and played in private, by and large – while Clough considered referee-baiting or even dissent taboo. 'There were two reasons for this,' said Frank Clark. 'One, Brian thought that was the right way to go about it; and, two, he thought we might get a better response from them if we treated them like human beings.' Trevor Francis, for whom Clough broke the British transfer record in paying Birmingham nearly £1 million in 1979, said: 'The first thing you were told when you came to the club was never to be involved with referees and I think most of the refs around at that time would say we were a pleasure to handle.' Given that they twice brought the European title back to Nottingham, which remains the smallest town ever to receive the honour, it did not appear to do Forest a great deal of harm. Just as Mourinho has his beliefs, so did Clough, and it is too early to compare their efficacy. If and when Mourinho has eclipsed Clough's achievements in England, once he has recovered from that Champions League reverse at the hands of Liverpool and left the restrained Rafael Benítez in his wake – if he can – judgement may be possible. But that is for the future.

Whatever next?

After the 2004–05 season had drawn to a close and the open-topped buses had been returned to their garages, there was a pause to reflect on Chelsea and how far the voyage of discovery might take them. Clearly it would depend on the man at the helm. By whom I mean José Mourinho. The requirement from Roman Abramovich was twofold and quite simple: he had to remain enthusiastic and ridiculously rich. Over the season, his enthusiasm had become undeniable (whatever the adventure's purpose, about which he remained silent) and his billions (as estimated by the media) had kept growing. We of modest means were bewildered by this. Did they not have taxation in Russia? Or was Abramovich benefiting from some form of relief for small businesses? It was beyond us. All we understood was that Chelsea would continue to have by far the biggest player budget in football. Which would entitle them to behave like the biggest club in the world and outbid the longer-recognised giants from Barcelona, Madrid, Milan and Manchester whenever a major talent became available. This was just the start, Mourinho had trumpeted after Chelsea had won the English championship for the first time in fifty years. So where would it all end?

Back in February 2005, a few days before Chelsea went to Cardiff to collect their first trophy under Mourinho, he told us his new team might not peak until his third season in charge. He might have been buying time – it is something coaches do, as Mourinho has scornfully remarked, in order to protect themselves from failure – but he explained his timetable fully. Because the gathering had been called in advance of the trip to Barcelona, he had been asked about the Champions League and, in particular, whether Chelsea at that stage were better equipped for it than his triumphant Porto of the previous season. 'We have better players,' he said, 'but Porto last year were a better team from the tactical point of view – because it was my third year with them. They knew everything I knew! They knew how to adapt just like this [he clicked his fingers]. They could change from system to system. I could start the game with 4–3–3, switch to 4–4–2, change back to 4–3–3. I could press high, put the block low.' But he had been at Chelsea only a matter of months. 'When we get to my third or fourth year, we can say this will be my best Chelsea team. So my contract with Chelsea is the right length.' It had a four-year span then. As well as being more lucrative now, it has been extended by a year.

Mourinho, even back in February, was already looking forward to a long pre-season, one more settled than his first, which had featured many comings and goings and the aftermath of the European Championship. 'I shall be working on things I don't want to work on now. Things must be done in phases and you cannot skip a phase. You have to do one after the other.' He was talking tactics and I asked if they had become more important than individual talent; the issue was topical after the triumphs of Porto and, at the European Championship, Greece. He replied: 'Although it is true that football is becoming more tactical, the fantastic player will always be able to decide a game with a piece of brilliance. And, if you have better players, you can have a better tactical organisation, because they are more intelligent, they understand the game better. It's just a question of whether they want to work for the team. Sometimes big players, if they won't work for the team, fail and smaller players with very good tactical organisation succeed. When you have both, you have the ideal.'

All the indications of his first season were that Mourinho's ability to organise and motivate a team had survived the step up in individual class. Petr Čech, Claude Makelele, Frank Lampard and Arjen Robben were arguably the world's leading players in their positions. John Terry and Damien Duff would have made it to many shortlists. Eidur Gudjohnsen could be said almost to have invented a role for himself; especially in the second half of the season, he had played beautifully. Joe Cole had fulfilled his potential. Yet the roll-call tells its own story. The majority of the squad had already been assembled by the club when Mourinho came. He merely fitted in the Portuguese trio and Didier Drogba (and the athletic Ivorian's hit-and-miss spells were to place a rare question mark against Mourinho's judgement). Furthermore, Mourinho had had to hoist Chelsea just one place up the Premiership table to make them champions. But it could not be denied: an improvement of fifteen points since the departure of Claudio Ranieri was conclusive and, if this and the Carling Cup constituted only a start, the mind boggles at the thought of where Chelsea might be when he is finished with them. In the summer of 2004, when Mourinho boarded Roman Abramovich's yacht for the meeting that was to culminate in his signing of that original contract, he was informed that the intention was to build the world's number-one football club. But I cannot imagine he will stop there.

Mourinho has created the odd hostage to fortune. Soon after meeting Abramovich he was shown a list that had been prepared for the Russian of top players from around the world and asked which he wanted. He rejected them one by one – the lot. It is reasonable to suppose the list included Wayne Rooney, and later Mourinho explained to the press that Chelsea had declined to challenge Manchester United for the teenager's signature 'because we already have players for that position'. Did he mean Drogba? And the little-used (and now sold to Atlético Madrid) Mateja Kežman? He may, even then, have been beginning to regret one element of this otherwise impressive declaration of independence on footballing matters.

There is no reason to believe he will want to leave Chelsea in the foreseeable future. He has told fellow coaches. He has told the Portuguese press: 'Nobody can give me a better championship, a better club, a better squad, better players, a better city, a country more passionate for football – nobody can give me a stadium completely full like I have here.' It was a sure sign of the years he spent with Sir Bobby Robson: he was speaking in lists. And the mid-season rumours of his flirtation with the idea of a move to Italy were never truly convincing. When he signed his enhanced contract, after the Champions League semi-final defeat at Liverpool had provided a moment's breather, he said something which, coming from the lips of such an avowed family man, carried far greater resonance than the mid-season hints: 'There is now no doubt that our lives are in London and that is important for my children.' He was then interviewed on *Match of the Day* after the title-celebration match against Charlton at Stamford Bridge. The opening shot was of Mourinho smiling. The interviewer, Ivan Gaskell, began:

'Chelsea gave you plenty to smile about this season.'

'Yes [Mourinho chuckled], but I'm a special guy, you know . . .'

'I've heard that somewhere before . . .'

'No, not in that way. Special guy in another way, you know.'

'In what way?'

'I'm not one hundred per cent happy with the season. I'm a bit disappointed. I would like to play in the Champions League final. I was very convinced of that, and people like me, when we don't reach our targets, I think we suffer more than . . . people who are happy with a few things.'

'Room for improvement, then?'

'It's not easy to improve a squad of champions, but we can improve a little bit. The supporters will have to try to improve. To support more the team, like some clubs in this country when they play at home.'

'And the press? Improve them too?'

'I think it's impossible to change.'

He did not look like a disappointed man. His smile was not so much broad as deep. It belied the pensiveness of his sentiments. But – and here the words of our psychoanalyst friend of a friend resound – Mourinho was not really trying to communicate with us. He was starting to condition his players for the next season (they seemed to get the message and responded with a superb win at Old Trafford three days later). And he was reminding the supporters that they, too, had been beaten by Liverpool.

Mourinho, according to his old university lecturer Manuel Sérgio, is 'the ultimate post-modern coach' and, while that is almost self-evidently overblown, there can be no argument with the view that the intellectual level of coaching in England has been raised by his presence. But post-modern? The global concept of coaching is not unique to Mourinho by any means, even if he and his staff have interpreted it brilliantly. He is not the first to play mind games, even if he is such a master of the dark arts that the Chelsea team went through the Barcelona and Bayern Munich episodes believing UEFA were victimising them and the opposition players – Barcelona's at any rate – being disrespectful. 'He really did create a siege mentality,' one player told me. But no; that could have been Ferguson. I tend to the view that Mourinho has not so much taken the coach's role on to a new level as put an exceptional amount of work into it. Even some of his best friends would concede that his outstanding qualities (the extraordinary charisma apart) are organis- ation and mental effort. 'Post-modern?' smiled one. 'You must remember that Manuel Sérgio is a philosopher.'

We have had long enough to observe how Mourinho goes about the job. We have learned how this extraordi- nary coach was formed. What we do not know is how long his success will endure. And where he will go once the Chelsea project matures. The answer may be:

nowhere. At the end of last season, after all, the longest-serving coach in the Premiership was one of his top-three companions, Sir Alex Ferguson, and the other, Arsène Wenger, was hot on the heels of Charlton's second-placed Alan Curbishley. But it is hard to see Mourinho as the dynastic type and it would be no surprise if, after a few years, he found himself once again restless for a fresh challenge. Given the mischievous nature of the forces that govern the movement and fortunes of football men, it might guide him back to Barcelona, where he was once so undervalued. That would surely appeal to him. The triumphant return of *El Traductor* – as *El Mister*. Or Real Madrid, where, quite apart from the thrill of the biannual *gran clásico* matches, he could square up to Barça on a daily basis through the media. What price, if we are to accept his wish to stay in England for a while, the ultimate challenge of Manchester United? For a man who has coached Benfica and Porto, the politics of such a move would hardly be too daunting.

The only fantasy Mourinho himself acknowledges, however, is that of leading his country. Not his country of residence, I hasten to add – 'when Sven-Göran Eriksson leaves,' he has said, 'that job should go to an Englishman' – but the country of his birth. He has told Andy Roxburgh: 'I would not like to retire without having been coach of Portugal.' And explained to the Portuguese newspaper *A Bola*: 'I want to do something that is for everybody. I want to help them be, one day, a little bit happier.' He spoke of how important a single international appearance had been for his father and added: 'My career as a coach will only make sense when, in a few years, I have the opportunity to train the national squad.' During his visit to Tel Aviv in March 2005, he put a rough timescale on it. 'I want to work for another thirteen years,' he said, 'and one thing is compulsory to me. I want to be manager of Portugal – when I want it. I want to manage my country for maybe two or four years, at a World Cup or European Championship. That leaves eleven or nine years in my career and I see myself staying in English football until then.' Unless, he added in Portugal after the season had finished, an opportunity arose to try a club in Italy. But the resolve to lead Portugal's national team remained fundamental, unaltered. So there you have it. From the man who does what it says on the tin.

So what will Mourinho do at the age of fifty-five, when, having stepped down as Portugal's coach following their success in the 2018 World Cup – perhaps the trophy will have been lifted by their ageing captain, Cristiano Ronaldo, once of Manchester United – he retires? Will he be content to sit reading on one of the beaches near Setúbal? Maybe for a month or two. But my guess is that, long in advance, he will have explored other avenues. Broader avenues than football can provide. While the Barcelona controversy was raging, Mourinho – as if to demonstrate there is no such thing as bad publicity – coincidentally became the new face of American Express in Europe and Asia. 'Why Asia?' he asked the people from the credit-card company, who told him he was as much an icon there as in Europe. He found that interesting and the trip to Israel, too, appeared to capture his imagination. 'When I have retired,' he said in Tel Aviv, 'when, in thirteen more years, I have finished with football, I can see myself one hundred per cent involved in human actions. I have always thought about problems in the Middle East and Africa, not just about football.' He has often denied any interest in politics, by which we can presume he means party politics, but there would surely be something to suit his talents at the United Nations. He has, after all, proved he can unite dressing rooms. But this is for the future too and many a football man has toyed with ideas of harnessing his power only to have second thoughts when the tiresome details of life in the slow lane become evident.

Mourinho went off for his summer holidays – the family made a beeline for Setúbal – around the time that England celebrated the eightieth wedding anniversary of Percy and Florence Arrowsmith, who were said to be the world's longest-married couple. Asked for any advice she could give people anxious to emulate the success of her relationship with Percy, the senior partner at 105, Florence, aged 100, replied: 'Never be afraid to say sorry.' Meanwhile Anders Frisk, a fugitive from a murkier world than the Arrowsmiths', was in Sweden watching his daughter ride her horse and his sons play football in the time his duties for an insurance company left free. A Champions League referee only four months earlier, his heart set on a career climax at the 2006 World Cup (for which he had already been invited by FIFA to train), Frisk now had no official involvement in football bar the education of young referees. Privately, declining countless interview requests, he awaited some sign of regret from Mourinho for the consequences, however unintended, of the Chelsea coach's questioning of his integrity in the Camp Nou. Mourinho's life had, of course, changed too. 'Especially my family life,' he had said. And I wondered how the Mourinhos would spend the days leading to their second festive season in London. Maybe José and Matilde would take their two children ice-skating in the little square just off the King's Road and be like any other happy family, their eyes shining under the Christmas lights and oblivious to the darkness beyond.

Index